FROM THE ESTATE OF
MISS MARJORIE GATES

D1159830

The Mulgrave Park Baptist Church
5656 Sebastion St.
Halifax, Canada
B3K 2K7

Baptists
Around the World

Baptists
Around the World
Theodore F. Adams

BROADMAN PRESS
Nashville, Tennessee

© Copyright 1967 · BROADMAN PRESS
All rights reserved

422–307

DEWEY DECIMAL CLASSIFICATION NUMBER: 286
Library of Congress catalog card number: 67–10306
Printed in the United States of America
14.N66KSP

To the members of the
First Baptist Church
Richmond, Virginia

With deep appreciation for
the privilege of being their
pastor and with gratitude for
their willingness to share
their pastor with other
BAPTISTS AROUND THE WORLD

Preface

> Blest be the tie that binds
> Our hearts in Christian love,
> The fellowship of kindred minds
> Is like to that above.

Baptists around the world are bound by many ties of faith and fellowship. The more than twenty-seven million Baptists differ in many ways, but with diversity there is a remarkable unity—"one Lord, one faith, one baptism, one God and Father of us all."

My wife and I count it a joy and privilege to have met many of our fellow Baptists in countries large and small on every continent. Everywhere we have been challenged and inspired by their devotion to Christ, even in the face of many difficulties.

The comparatively few we can tell about in this little book are representative of many more who are just as consecrated. We are grateful to the friends who were willing for us to share their stories with you. We trust their faith and spirit will inspire you and others, as they have inspired us.

We are also grateful to the members of the historic church we have served for more than thirty years, for their willingness to share their pastor with others around the world, and to my faithful secretary, Emma Hutchins, who read my writing and that of many others and typed the manuscript.

It is our hope that this book will not only tell the reader about Baptists and what they believe and do but will also lead many to want to know more about Baptists around the world and the Christ they love and serve.

THEODORE F. ADAMS

First Baptist Church
Richmond, Virginia, USA

Contents

The Mulgrave Park Baptist Church
5656 Sebastion St.
Halifax, Canada
B3K 2K7

AFRICA

AFRICA

Liberia

William R. Tolbert, Jr.

"I commit myself as a servant of God and as an instrument in his hands. I feel that I have been summoned by God." These words were spoken by William R. Tolbert, Jr., in Miami Beach, Florida, in 1965, immediately after his election as president of the Baptist World Alliance. He is the first Negro to serve in this capacity.

Dr. Tolbert is a minister, a businessman, and a political leader. Ordained as a gospel minister in 1953, he has served a number of churches in his native Africa, as well as serving as president of the Liberian Baptist Convention and as a vice-president of the Baptist World Alliance.

He is also a farmer, chairman of the Board of Directors of the Bank of Liberia, and member of a number of other corporations and institutions.

For eight years, he served as a member of the House of Representatives in Liberia. In 1951, he was elected vice-president of the country and president of the Senate for three succeeding terms.

Some idea of what his election as president of the Baptist World Alliance can mean to the work of Christ can be seen in the following statement. Addressing the Commission on Evan-

13

gelism and Missions at the Miami meeting, he said: "Christianity is on trial. The church must show it is dynamic in modern life. One way we can do this is to let the light of the gospel shine through the whole life. Too often we have isolated our Christianity into one area of our lives and operated on different principles in the areas of economics, politics, and social life. Christian morality must not remain outside; it must be a part of every area of life."

Who is this interesting and remarkable man, and how did he come to such a high place in his country and in the Baptist world?

He was born in Bensonville, Liberia, in 1913, attended public schools, and graduated from what is now the University of Liberia. His wife, Victoria, is a daughter of a distinguished Liberian jurist and politician. The couple have two sons and six daughters of their own, and an adopted son.

The story of the adopted son is a moving one and reveals even more of the character and spirit of Dr. and Mrs. Tolbert. Some years ago, while making an official visit to a village far from the capital of Liberia, Dr. Tolbert noticed a great crowd ahead of him. Sensing considerable excitement, he followed along and to his amazement found that several men were carrying a young boy in a crude cage.

Greatly handicapped because he had been born without arms, the lad was terrified—and with good reason. The village witch doctor had ordered that he be sacrificed.

Dr. Tolbert immediately instructed the men to put the boy down. He unfastened the cage, helped the lad out, and asked if he would like to come and live in his home and be his son. The boy could hardly believe his ears but smiled through his tears and agreed at once.

That boy has now become a fine young man and is at Ricks Institute, a splendid Southern Baptist mission school in Liberia. He is an active member of the church and is able to carry on as a happy, intelligent, and dedicated citizen of his country —all because W. R. Tolbert practices what he preaches and, like his Lord, goes about doing good.

Many honors and distinctions have come to Dr. Tolbert, including an honorary doctorate of civil law from the University of Liberia. He has represented his country at the United Nations and has visited many other nations as well. He has often represented the president of Liberia at such occasions as the coronation of Queen Elizabeth II, the inauguration of President Harry S. Truman, the coronations of Pope John XXIII and Pope Paul VI, and the funeral of President John F. Kennedy. A number of nations have given him high awards in recognition of his distinguished service to his own government and theirs.

But how does this man happen to be who and where he is? The answer dates back to Dr. Tolbert's first visit to Richmond, Virginia. The place he wanted to visit, above all others, was First Baptist Church. As he entered the sanctuary, he asked, "May I pray?" He knelt at the steps leading up to the pulpit and prayed very earnestly, thanking God for the First Baptist Church and for all that it had meant to him and to his country. Apart from the events of 150 years ago in the Baptist church in Richmond he probably would not have been there, nor would he now be the president of the Baptist World Alliance.

The story goes back to April 26, 1815, when, in the First Baptist Church in Richmond, the Richmond Baptist African Mission Society was organized. This action grew out of the visit of Luther Rice as a representative of the Triennial Baptist

Convention, formed in Philadelphia in 1814. Rice had just come back from Burma to arouse new interest in missions among Baptists and to raise money to support the Judsons in Burma.

The Richmond Baptist African Mission Society had as two of its most faithful members Collin Teague, a saddler and harness maker, and Lott Cary, a foreman in a large tobacco warehouse. The Society met regularly for mission study and prayer, and, through the Triennial Convention, they made generous gifts each year to mission work in Africa.

In 1819, Cary and Teague offered themselves to the Triennial Convention for mission service. After their acceptance, they devoted themselves to continuing study, and in 1820 were publicly ordained to the gospel ministry in the First Baptist Church in Richmond. Shortly after this, there was formed in the home of one of the deacons in the church a seven-member "African Baptist Church." The members were Rev. and Mrs. Lott Cary, Rev. and Mrs. Collin Teague and their son Hillary, and Mr. and Mrs. Joseph Langford.

Lott Cary preached his farewell sermon to the church in 1821. A few days later the little church sailed, with other colonists, to Liberia. There they founded the Liberian Baptist Mission. That church, the next year, was reorganized as the Providence Baptist Church of Monrovia, Liberia. From this small beginning, Baptist work and influence grew and spread in Liberia. Lott Cary served not only as a missionary but also as a representative of the colonization government. Hillary Teague later became a pastor in Monrovia and was also editor of the *Liberia Herald*.

Small wonder that William Tolbert knelt to thank God when first he visited the church in Richmond. From that church, and supported by that church, had gone the Baptist pioneers who took to his native land the faith he now represents so well. Truly, the seeds sown so faithfully long ago have brought forth good fruit.

Evidence of the kind of man Baptists have chosen to lead them for five years is seen in the following words from his acceptance address at the Eleventh Baptist World Congress at Miami Beach, Florida, where he was formally installed as leader of Baptists around the world:

You have, my dear brothers and sisters, made a gracious choice of me to serve as president of this august body. I do not doubt that you realize in so doing, by human standards, you have not chosen your best, as I recognize that among you my superiors are many. But I go on record in boldly asserting that you have summoned one from your midst to serve who is an humble servant of Almighty God, and who will ever seek his guidance and endeavor to do his will. To him first I owe my complete allegiance and unswerving loyalty, and then to you. Thus, to our great God, and to you, I now with dedication pledge my services to the limit of my resources.

As far as I am concerned, geographical limitations, occasioned by nature and fixed by man, and racial distinctions, caused by skin pigmentation, vanish into nothingness in the great economy and plan of our God. With me there is neither east nor west, north nor south. There exists, as far as human objects appearing within the range of my vision, neither white, black, red, yellow, or brown. We are all inhabitants of one world—God's world. . . .

Ours is a restless and changing world in need of patience, human understanding, faith in one another, tolerance, sympathy, the spirit of forgiveness, good will, and, above all, love. The barriers erected out of misunderstanding, selfishness, personal expediences, intolerance, conceit, skepticism, jealousy, envy, bigotry, prejudice, and hate must be demolished. We can and must take an active role in occasioning this to the glory of God and the peace and security of our world.

Brethren, let us love one another! Thus we truly identify ourselves as the children of God and fulfil the law of Christ.

Lagos, Nigeria

J. T. Ayorinde

"Who knows what this boy may become?" is the real meaning of the name given to Tanimola Ayorinde, when he was born into a heathen family at Abeokuta in 1907. He still bears on his face the marks of the Nigerian tribe to which he belongs, but he bears in his life and in his heart the marks of a true man of God.

How did all this come to pass? It is a strange and moving story.

One day when he was playing with other boys in the dusty streets of Abeokuta, Miss Olive Edens, a Southern Baptist missionary, asked the boys to let her tell them some stories. They were interested and soon were attending a Bible study class. Sensing that Tanimola was a boy of great promise, Miss Edens arranged for him to go to the Baptist Boys' School in Abeokuta. He soon became a Christian, as a result of Miss Edens' teaching. One of the real regrets of his life is that his parents both died while he was still in school and before he was able to do anything to help them accept Christ. His brother is now a Christian, and his sister who died some years ago, although married to a Muslim, was also a Christian.

His parents opposed his seeking more education, but he was

so determined that, with Miss Edens' help, he left Abeokuta to study for five years at the Baptist college and seminary at Ogbomosho. Graduating there in 1927, he went back to teach at the Boys' School in Abeokuta until 1938.

Meanwhile, a lovely Yoruba girl, the fourth child of Mr. and Mrs. John Agboola, was growing as a Christian. Mobola attended primary school and later the Girls' School in Abeokuta. After graduation she continued to teach and while there met and married James T. Ayorinde. Mobola, like many Yoruba women, is a clever businesswoman and a skilled trader, but above all else she is a devoted Christian and dedicated servant of the Lord Jesus Christ.

Mobola writes of herself: "When God calls, he qualifies, and when he qualifies, he sends. God has really called me, qualified me, and sent me to work among my own people. . . . Being childless disturbed me a lot in the beginning of our married life. We very much wanted children, but in vain. Finally, we realized that it was God's will for us to remain childless so that we might serve him better. Knowing this, I buried my will in the will of God and surrendered my whole life to him. Today I have so many children in Christ who gladden my heart. Having no children has given me more time to serve my Lord and Saviour."

The Ayorindes early realized the need for more training. In 1938, God opened the way for them to study at Virginia Union University in Richmond, Virginia. While they were studying, Tanimola contracted tuberculosis. For a time it seemed that he would have to give up the work he loved, but after a few months' hospitalization and proper care he was fully healed and the disease has never troubled him since. He received his B.A. degree from Virginia Union in 1940 and his M.A. in Religious Education from Oberlin College in 1942. Oberlin College later conferred upon him the honorary D.D. degree.

When Tanimola was a student at Virginia Union University he was asked to write an article on "How I Became a Christian." He told about the Sunday School class in Abeokuta taught by Miss Edens. The article, with his picture, was published in the *Religious Herald,* the Virginia Baptist state paper.

Mrs. Jenkins, mother of L. Howard Jenkins, then president of the Foreign Mission Board of the Southern Baptist Convention, read the article while in a Richmond hospital. When her son visited her, she expressed a desire to meet the Nigerian student.

Dr. Ayorinde says that during the visit, Mrs. Jenkins asked, "Did you know Miss Edens?" When he answered, "Yes, very well," she queried, "Do you consider it worthwhile for someone to spend his money on missions?"

Once again he answered yes, pointing out that he was a product of mission work and that as such he was a living testimony for the worthwhileness of supporting missions around the world. "If no one had cared, I would not now have the chance I have. I am not the only one whose life has been touched by the work of missions. There are many, many others."

When he finished, Mrs. Jenkins said with a radiant look on her face, "I am happy now. Will you read the Bible and pray for me?"

In his prayer, he thanked God for missionaries in foreign lands and prayed for Mrs. Jenkins as well. After the prayer, Mrs. Jenkins called her son and said, "Howard, I want you and this young man to be good friends. See that while in this country he is well cared for." There began then a friendship that has endured through the years.

Only later did Dr. Ayorinde learn that when Howard Jenkins was a boy he was very sick. His mother had prayed and vowed that she would do something special for the Lord if the boy's life were spared. Her son recovered and in keeping with her promise, Mrs. Jenkins undertook to support a missionary in a foreign land. That missionary was Olive Edens, who, by the grace of God, led Tanimola to Christ and helped him to come to America, where he could minister to the donor herself in her last illness in a Richmond hospital.

Shortly after the Ayorindes returned to Nigeria, Mobola was taken seriously ill. Her friends in Nigeria wanted her to come to America for skilled treatment. When the Baptist women of Virginia learned of her need, they immediately cabled that she was to come at once. She left so quickly that there was some trouble with her travel documents, but she finally reached Richmond. As we sat one day at lunch at the College Inn on the campus of Virginia Union University, she told us of her experience and about her difficulties with the immigration authorities when she landed in New York alone. She said, "I just shut my eyes and prayed, 'Lord, I am your child. I am in your hands. I don't know what to do, so you take care of things for me that I might go back to Nigeria well and serve my people there'." This simple childlike faith was rewarded. All the difficulties were cleared up at the port of entry, and in a short time she was well and strong again.

On her return to Nigeria, she and her husband gave themselves wholeheartedly, not only to the work in their own land, but across Africa. Dr. Ayorinde served as pastor of the Owu Baptist Church for a year or two and then became pastor of the outstanding First Baptist Church in Lagos, Nigeria. He served as president of the Nigerian Baptist Convention, 1950–55, and as a vice-president of the Baptist World Alliance, 1955–60, and continued as a member of the Executive Committee of the world organization of Baptists. He has been invited by Baptists to preach in special evangelistic campaigns in several other countries around the world.

Mobola serves as leader of women's work in Africa for the Women's Department of the Alliance, and in this capacity has traveled over most of Africa, rallying African women to the service of Christ.

When we visited Nigeria in 1956, we spent some time in Lagos. It was my privilege to preach in Dr. Ayorinde's church and to see him baptize a large group who had confessed their faith in Christ as Saviour. One night we went to dinner in the Ayorinde home in a little apartment adjacent to the church. When Tanimola first suggested the possibility, Mobola demurred and said, "Oh, I couldn't entertain them. Our home is so humble and I would not know how to serve them."

Tanimola replied, "When I was in Richmond, I put my feet under Dr. Adams' table and now that he is in Lagos, he is going to put his feet under my table." So, we and a missionary couple were invited to dinner. Mobola overcame her nervousness and was a splendid hostess. We had a memorable time together.

When I. N. Patterson resigned as secretary of the Nigerian Baptist Convention and retired from mission service, Nigerian Baptists chose Dr. Ayorinde as associate general secretary and then as general secretary. This is the first time a Nigerian has headed the work of this Convention, but the Lord had Tanimola ready when the time came and he was needed.

Brethren other than Baptists also recognized his worth. For a number of years he served as chairman of the Nigerian Broadcasting Corporation, in charge of all radio and television in

AFRICA   23

Nigeria. This called for a number of trips to London for conferences with the British Broadcasting Corporation. From a young lad on the streets of Abeokuta to one of the leading citizens of his own land, Dr. Ayorinde is ready to serve God and his country in this new day of independence. Surely, he was well named—"Who knows what this *boy* will become?"

Cape Town, South Africa

Glyn Tudor

The "death march" was on in Poland. The
Germans, in 1945, were desperately trying to keep their prisoners ahead of the invading army that was slowly but surely
driving them back. Food and water were scarce, and men who
dropped out were brutally treated and left behind, but some
struggled on.

In one group of prisoners was Chaplain Glyn Tudor of South
Africa. This is the way he describes the experience:

"Perhaps the most meaningful time of my life was spent in
active service during the war, when my spiritual experience
was tested and tried as never before or since. It was a time
when, and especially on the 'death march,' I realized how ex-
pendable man is in man's estimation, but how infinitely precious to God is the least of his own. At a time when my own
faith reached a low ebb, the Lord seemed to become more and
more tender toward me, until he brought me to see and to
appreciate what it was all about. He indeed 'tempered the wind
to the shorn lamb,' resulting in an infinitely stronger faith and
wider vision than ever before."

Glyn Tudor today is the strong and vital pastor of the Ob-
servatory Baptist Church in Cape Town, South Africa. Physi-

cally, he gives no evidence of the agony of the "death march," but his spiritual life impresses all who hear him or come to know him. Here is a man with a vital faith, tested and tried, whom God has prepared for such a time as this in South Africa.

Glyn was born in Wales, in 1913, and had his early scholastic and theological training there. Later he studied at the university in South Africa, after being called from Wales to become pastor of Springs Baptist Church in the Transvaal. He now holds a B.A. degree from the University of Natal. Since 1954, he and his wife and three children have made their home in beautiful Cape Town.

When the war began, Glyn went into active service with the South African Forces in Libya, North Africa, and Egypt. He was captured by the Germans in 1942, and was a prisoner of war for three years in Italy, Germany, and Poland. After the "death march" and his eventual release, he stayed on in England for a time to regain health and strength.

In 1946 he returned to his homeland, where he resumed his service as a pastor. He has also been a member of the Executive Committee of the Baptist Union and of the South African Baptist Missionary Society, and served as president 1959–60.

He attended the Baptist Youth World Conference in Rio de Janeiro in 1953 and in Toronto in 1958, and was also present at the Pan-African Youth Conference in Nigeria in 1959. He has been a valued member of the Executive Committee of the Baptist World Alliance and shared in a study conference with members of that body in Ruschlikon in 1958. He has participated in the World congresses in Rio and in Miami Beach.

It was not easy for Glyn to represent South Africa in the Pan-African Youth Conference in Nigeria, for many young people from Central and East Africa spoke openly and strongly about their concern with race relations in South Africa. Since 1954, Glyn has been the Baptist Union Representative on the South African Institute of Race Relations. He has tried his best to help solve the difficult problems faced in South Africa. Speaking about this grave problem, he says:

Living in South Africa these many years, I am naturally vitally concerned about race relations and would very much like to study more in this particular field, so I can be of more use to the Lord along these lines. Our South African setup is, of course, extremely delicate and is not comparable with any other situation in the world.

Our Baptist Union is not silent where there is injustice or any form of oppression of voiceless groups. I have personally worked with the Christian Council and the Institute of Race Relations in this direction. We will not enter the political field as such, but I have worked with other interdenominational bodies, particularly those of an evangelical witness.

As chairman of the Cape Town Evangelical Christian Council, I have been responsible for bringing to South Africa a number of well-known evangelical personalities who have found great acceptance, not only with English-speaking churches, but also with our Afrikaans brethren in the Dutch Reformed Church. I am all for international, interracial, and interdenominational cooperation, provided my own stand for the evangelical faith and witness, the truth of the Scriptures, and our Baptist heritage is not compromised in any way.

In these tense times in South Africa and in the world, when the problem of race is one of the paramount issues confronting Christians, how good it is that in the providence of God, Glyn Tudor survived the "death march" and is ready to serve his Lord and his brethren in his homeland. His faith is tried and true and he is fully committed to his Lord. We can say of him as was said of another long ago, "Thou art come to the kingdom for such a time as this."

Rhodesia

W. M. S. President

      We have met the presidents of many Woman's Missionary Societies in the homeland and around the world. One we remember especially lives in a little village in Rhodesia.

She was introduced to us as the president of the Woman's Missionary Society of the little Baptist group that worshiped in this village. We were invited into her home, which was spotlessly clean. On the floor were mats that she had made herself. As a matter of fact, she was outside weaving another mat when we arrived.

On a small shelf on one side of the single room were her cooking utensils and dishes. There were only a few pans and spoons and a minimum of enamelware dishes. Some Christian pictures hung on the walls. Only a few pieces of clothing were to be seen. It was a meager wardrobe at best for a family, and we wondered what would happen when bad weather came. There was one single bed on another side of the room. It is customary for the husband to sleep on the one bed. The wife and children sleep on mats on the floor.

In a little fenced-in enclosure adjacent to the house, this good woman cooked the evening meal over an open fire. Her utensils

27

were simple—one big pot on a tripod and one or two smaller pots on stones close to the fire. From time to time she would stir the stew with a huge metal spoon.

We talked about her Lord and ours. Her face beamed as she spoke of her faith and of what the missionary and the little church meant to her and her family. A Christian for several years, she had been seeking to win her whole village to Christ.

She was chosen as president of the Woman's Missionary Society because she was the only woman in the village who could read. In her childhood she had received a limited education, but the other women had none. It was her responsibility to lead the meetings of the Society, to teach the other women the Bible, and to read to them the prepared lesson, and to tell them about Christian work in their own and other lands. Without her, the missionary would be greatly handicapped. With her, the work is going forward among the women of this village.

A little later we visited the school and met the Christian teacher in charge. We also visited the village church where the missionary serves as pastor.

Some new and better homes were being built by the government to replace some of the older thatched-roof houses. They had a covered porch for outdoor cooking and two rooms for each family. The polygamists would still have to get along with a one-room, thatched-roof house for each wife.

As we drove away, the one outstanding memory of our visit to this little village was of this devoted and dedicated Christian woman. Faithfully caring for her family, she is making the best of the little she has. Loyal to her church and her Lord, she is striving to win others to Christ and to teach her children and her sisters in Christ the truths of God. "Of such is the kingdom of heaven."

EUROPE

EUROPE

England

Ronald Bell

One day in London, England, I presented my card at the office of the Temperance Permanent Building Society. The clerk said, "Just a moment and I will see whether Mr. Bell can see you." Very soon I was ushered into the beautifully appointed office of Ronald Bell, managing director of the Society. He greeted me as an old friend, warmly and heartily, and asked what I was doing there. I replied, "I am here in London for a few days on Baptist business and I just wanted to come by and see you and thank you for all you did for the Jubilee Congress in London."

Ron Bell had served as chairman of the Committee on Arrangements for the Ninth Baptist World Congress in London in 1955. It was at this Congress that we celebrated our Golden Jubilee—fifty years of cooperative fellowship and service in the Baptist World Alliance. Ronald Bell had gladly assumed that heavy responsibility. The Baptists of the world were the beneficiaries of his vision and dedication. With fine business judgment and with great attention to detail, he helped to arrange to care for the thousands of visiting Baptists during the busy tourist season. He arranged for scores of meetings all over London and for some outstanding sessions in Royal Albert Hall. The closing session, addressed by Billy Graham, in a great outdoor stadium was a memorable experience for all who had the privilege of sharing in it.

He took me to lunch at his favorite restaurant near his office. There I noted his friendly relationships with those who served us, for here was a man who had come from humble beginnings and had not forgotten what it meant to be poor and what it means to serve others.

After lunch we went back to his office, where he took time only to care for a few pressing matters and then said, "Now, we'll get my car and go for a drive." That day I saw some of London that I had never seen before. We visited an old, old church near his home, as well as the church where he and his wife were faithful members. We had a quiet tea in his home and later he and his wife took me to dinner at a beautiful old English inn.

As we talked about Baptist life and work in England, I was grateful to God for laymen like this. He had won his way in business, but his supreme joy was in serving Christ and his church in ways too numerous to mention.

Little did I realize when I left Ron that day that he was soon to be stricken with a severe illness that was followed by almost total blindness. He could read only by holding a paper close to his eyes, but the directors of his business had such confidence in him that they said, "If your doctor says that you can continue for even a few hours a day, we want you to stay on as director of the business." This he did, although he had to give up many of his other activities and concentrate only on his business, his home, and his church. All who knew him were impressed with his quiet acceptance of these limitations. His faith was so deep and true that he was able to bear it all with the assurance that has helped so many, "I can do all things through Christ which strengtheneth me."

After some years of limited service, death came very suddenly. When his wife and his lawyer were going through the papers he had left, they found that he had given careful instructions about his funeral service and burial. He wanted Ernest Payne, an old friend and leader of the Baptists of England, to conduct the service, with his own pastor assisting. He asked that the congregation join in singing the hymn "The King of Love My Shepherd Is." What comfort the twenty-third Psalm must have brought to him as he literally walked for a number of years through the valley of the shadow of death, fearing no evil, for he knew the Lord was with him.

He trusted, too, in the promise, "I will dwell in the house of the Lord forever." At the end of the instructions about the funeral service, he had penned these simple but significant words: "Going home—not to the unknown."

Those of us who knew and loved Ronald Bell are grateful not only for his life of dedicated Christian service in days of opportunity, vigor, and responsibility but also for the witness he bore in times of trial, pain, and distress. Surely, he has gone home, not to the unknown, but to an even more real fellowship with the Christ he loved and served so well—in the "house not made with hands, eternal in the heavens" (2 Cor. 5:1).

France

Henri Vincent

Henri Vincent and I first met at what was then Rochester Theological Seminary in Rochester, New York. His father and mine had both attended this school, and we soon became fast friends. His son John, who is now studying at the seminary at Ruschlikon in Zurich, Switzerland, is the fourth generation Baptist preacher in this remarkable family.

Henri's grandfather, Francois, was converted while a young man, through the ministry of a visiting evangelist in the little village where he lived in northern France. Henri's father, Philemon, was trained as a Baptist pastor in both the United States and France and served faithfully in Paris as pastor of the Avenue du Maine Baptist Church.

Philemon was pleased when his son Paul, who had accepted Christ earlier, felt called to become a Baptist pastor. Paul studied in Rochester on a scholarship given by a woman in the United States who was interested in educating pastors for service in other lands. It was a sad day when Paul was killed in Belgium in World War I. The father's heart was heavy. However, Henri decided to follow his brother in the ministry, and in 1919 went to Rochester to enrol in the seminary. After his graduation in 1922, Henri went back to France where he served as assistant to his father in the Avenue du Maine Baptist Church.

Henri was married in 1928 to a Baptist girl from northern France who belonged to one of the churches his grandfather founded. They have been blessed with five children. Henri became pastor of the Avenue du Maine Church in 1929 and served there until 1952, when he founded the Rue de Lille Baptist Church and became its pastor. In 1936, the Baptists of France elected him as their president and he served in this capacity until 1963, when they made him honorary president.

World War II interrupted his ministry in the church, and he served as one of the few Protestant chaplains in the French Army. When the Allies retreated to Dunkirk, many escaped, but Henri was left with the wounded in the hospital there. When the Germans entered the city, he was taken prisoner but was soon told by his captors, "The war will be over in a few days. You might as well go home. We don't want to keep you a prisoner."

"So," says Henri with a smile, "I went home and promptly joined the underground in Paris."

He served in the underground chiefly as a helper to the Jews who were seeking to escape from Nazi persecution and terror. This was perfectly natural because he had started a Jewish mission in 1936 and directed it until the war. Many Jewish refugees now came to this mission seeking a hiding place or some way of escape from certain death at the hands of the Nazis.

One day a frightened Jewish woman came seeking a place of refuge. She was hidden for a few days until a place could be found for her in a village some distance from Paris. When all the arrangements were made, Vincent told the woman just

where to go and how to get to the village and the place of
safety. The woman, however, was terrified and would not go
alone. She finally agreed to go if the pastor would travel with
her. This was a tremendous risk because if he were caught
with her it would mean death for both. However, with calm
courage he made the journey, took the Jewish woman to a
place of refuge, and then came back to Paris to help others.

One day Henri was told by a fellow member of the underground that in a cafe he had overheard two Nazi officers speaking about "that Baptist pastor" and saying that his apartment
was to be searched because he was hiding a Jew there. Vincent
quickly made his way home and a Jewish refugee who was
there was soon secure in another hiding place. The pastor was
sure, however, that his apartment would be searched.

The next day was Sunday. When he and his wife returned
from the preaching service at the church, the police were there,
and the whole apartment was in disorder. They had searched
every room, not only for a refugee, but for any papers that
might incriminate the minister. Papers from all the drawers of
his desk were spread out on the dining table. When he entered
and found the searchers, almost involuntarily Henri's hand
went to his coat pocket, for hidden in the pocket was a set of
false papers he had obtained that day for another Jew.

Spotting his action, the Nazi captain said, "What do you
have in your pocket? Put all your papers on the table." Henri
quickly complied and put everything on the table in front of
him. He smiled as he told me about it later. "Fortunately, my
church had paid me that day and the check was on the top of
the papers." The Nazi chief picked up the check and began to
question him rapidly: "Where did this money come from? Who
really pays you? Whom do you work for? Who are you really

serving?" The questions were asked so quickly that Henri could
not answer them all at once. With impatience, the Nazi chief
said, "You will come with me at once to the office." With a
smile of relief, Henri walked out of his apartment with the
police, leaving on the table behind him the false papers that
would have certainly sent him to prison! At the office he was
able to explain the check satisfactorily and was soon released
to go home, where he continued to serve his Lord and his
church and Jewish refugees.

One day after the war, I preached in the Avenue du Maine
Church. As a Jewish girl went by us after the service, Henri
said, "Remind me to tell you about her sister."

When the crowd had gone, I said, "Please tell me about the
Jewish girl."

"She and her sister came to us as refugees during the war.
We hid the two girls securely in different villages in homes of
believers. One day the police, seeking someone else, went to
the home of one of the believers and found the sister of the
girl you met. She was taken quickly to Paris and put in a truck
to be shipped to the gas chambers in Germany. Somehow as
she rode through the streets she managed to write a note on a
scrap of paper and address it to me. She dropped the bit of
paper through a crack in the truck. Someone later picked it up,
saw my address, and brought it to me. On it she had written,
"Do not fear for me. I do not know where I am going, but my
faith is sufficient and God will see me through to the end."

Such was the faith of one whom Vincent had won to Christ,
not only by his preaching, but by the witness of his life and
his willingness to risk his own life to save others and to give
them freedom.

Vincent's activities have gone far beyond his own work in

France. In 1948, he was one of the men who helped to start the European Baptist Federation that has drawn the Baptists of Europe closer together in faith and fellowship and service. In 1954, he helped to organize the European Baptist Missionary Society to replace older missionary bodies of several countries who could not maintain separate societies.

The Society began with just German and French representatives, but seven other nations are now represented: Switzerland, Italy, Spain, Yugoslavia, Finland, Belgium, and Austria. Vincent has served as president from the beginning. The Society has two fields in the Cameroun with nineteen missionaries from Germany, France, Switzerland, Italy, and Finland.

At the World Congress of the Baptist World Alliance in 1960 he was elected a vice-president. In a special convocation there in Rio de Janeiro, Ralph Johnson, president of Berkley Divinity School, conferred the honorary D.D. degree on Henri Vincent, a good minister of Jesus Christ.

When I think of my friend Henri Vincent, and the quiet and devoted way in which he has served his Lord and others, like Paul who was cheered by his brethren long ago, "I thank God and take courage."

Germany

Jakob Meister

       Finally reaching Berlin, late in World War II, the Russian soldiers were determined to ravage the city, just as the Nazis had ravaged Stalingrad. One day, soon after the occupation began, Russian soldiers knocked at the door of the Bethel Deaconess House in Berlin. Inside, the deaconesses were caring for the sick and needy, but there were also many women who had gone there as a place of refuge.

The director of the Deaconess House, Jakob Meister, opened the door. The Russians demanded entrance, but Meister barred the way. He alone stood between the occupying forces and the many women within. Showing them his Swiss passport, he demanded that they go away. The Russians were a bit taken aback by his boldness and by the Swiss passport, but one soldier fired a shot which made a hole in the wall. When water gushed forth, the soldiers beat a hasty retreat. Smiling as he told about it, Dr. Meister said: "Perhaps they thought it was something of a miracle that water came through the hole. They did not know they had merely punctured a tank that held part of our emergency water supply."

It was a miracle that the women within were spared. In the providence of God, the deaconesses were able to go on caring for the sick and the needy, while much of Berlin was ravaged.

The man who stood at that door and saved those within was certainly God's man for that hour and for many days to come. He guided and protected the work of the Deaconess House all through the days of the Russian occupation and still later when the American forces took over, after Berlin was divided into occupation zones. In the same brave and smiling way he had guided the work through the days of the Nazis and all through the bitter experiences and bombings of World War II.

Jakob Meister was born in Zurich, Switzerland. He accepted Christ as Saviour and Lord when he was fifteen years old and was baptized on Pentecost in his home church in Zurich.

He was the only son of the family and his father intended that he should take over the family business. Young Jakob, however, had other ideas. He felt called to the ministry and for the next four years attended the Baptist Seminary in Hamburg, Germany. After graduation he served as pastor of a small Baptist church in Danzig, then in eastern Germany but now a part of Poland. In 1917, he married Augusta Ruhrmann, who through the years has been his faithful co-worker and partner. From 1919 to 1928, he served the Baptist church in Konigsberg, at that time the capital of East Germany but now Kaliningrad in Soviet Russia. At that time there were sixteen thousand Baptists in the province.

In 1928, Dr. Meister was called back to Zurich to be the pastor of his home church. It was not easy to give up the work in East Germany where he and his wife were much loved, but he followed the call of duty and went back to his homeland. There the Lord richly blessed their work in the church and Jakob also served for a time as president of the Baptist Union of Switzerland.

In 1935, Dr. Meister was called back to Germany to serve as pastor and director of Bethel House in Berlin. Baptists in other lands are not too familiar with Baptist deaconesses, but in Germany they are familiar figures and highly trained and dedicated servants of Christ.

Bethel House is the headquarters for 398 sisters who serve as deaconesses in churches, hospitals, and many kinds of social work. A number of them serve as assistants in churches, but most of them serve in hospitals and homes for the aged. Their worth was truly demonstrated during the difficult years of World War II and the occupation that followed. At that time, Bethel deaconesses were serving in thirty Baptist churches in Berlin and the suburbs. Not only did they care for the needy in the churches, but also the sick and wounded. They were there and ready when the stream of refugees from the East began to pour into Berlin. They were of immense help in relief work and assisted hundreds who were homeless and needy, and often desperate for a place to live and food to eat.

When the Baptist World Congress met in Copenhagen in 1947, just after the war, refugees, as well as representatives of countries that had been at war, attended. The German who spoke for his country in the Roll Call of the Nations could hardly say what was in his heart. Finally, with deep emotion, he said that it meant much to him and his fellow Germans to see their flag once again in the family of nations and to be received as Christian brothers by those with whom they had been at war.

Those who came from the West were appalled by the needs they saw. At the call of the Baptist World Alliance Relief Committee, those who were attending the Congress went through their bags and brought all they could spare of clothing, soap, and other necessities, and piled it on huge tables. A call went out for money for relief and much of this was spent in Berlin through the Deaconess House and Dr. Meister. Thousands of refugees of all races, creeds, and nationalities were cared for through Baptist World Relief in many different countries. The Deaconess House was a focal point for this work in vital and beleaguered Berlin.

From 1946 to 1956, Dr. Meister also served as president of the Baptist Union of Germany. His fellowship with German Baptists and his Swiss citizenship were of great help in arranging for Alliance relief work throughout the country and for the rebuilding of many Baptist churches. Other gifts made it possible for a number of refugee congregations to build new homes and churches. Truly, God had another man ready just when and where he was needed.

Although Dr. Meister has retired from active service and now makes his home in his beloved Switzerland, it is good to know that the Lord's work goes on in the Meister name. His two sons continue to serve. Theophil, the elder, is an x-ray physician serving in two hospitals. Claus, the younger, is a professor at the Baptist Theological Seminary in Ruschlikon.

Dr. Meister says the secret of his life is contained in a simple sentence given him by Pastor Edward Scheve, a Baptist pioneer in Germany and Switzerland, when he was baptized: "Only the grace of God is able to make our life precious for time and eternity."

Poland

Alexander Kircun

The city of Warsaw, Poland, was more than 90 percent destroyed during World War II. The thousands of Jews who lived in "the ghetto" were among the first and last victims of Nazi occupation and destruction. They knew they could expect only death, so they fought to the bitter end. The devastation was so complete that when the time came for rehabilitation, the ruins were simply flattened out to form a burial place for the thousands who had died.

Over the ruins of the Jewish section of the city, the Jews of the world erected a majestic and moving monument. Figures in metal tell the story of the heroism of those who fought and endured to the end—young and old, men and women. The marble in the monument was originally ordered in Sweden by Hitler to be used for a triumphant monument to himself when he conquered the Scandinavian countries, as he expected to do. When the war was over and Hitler was dead, this same marble was obtained by Jewish leaders and used in the monument they erected as their tribute to the Jews who died in Warsaw. The very marble Hitler thought would glorify him stands instead as a silent tribute to those who, at his orders, died for their faith and their families.

The little Baptist congregation in Warsaw had been reduced by the war from about four hundred to only fourteen. Alexander Kircun, president of the Polish Baptist Convention, and his family had stayed in the city all through the tragic devastation. Other pastors had gone to the West, seeking peace and security, but Kircun and his wife and children stayed on to serve the Lord and his people. After the war, the little congregation worshiped in a crowded upstairs apartment.

In the summer of 1958, a group of Baptists from America and many European countries stood amid the rubble in one section of Warsaw. The occasion was the centennial of Baptists in Poland. The minister of religion in the Polish Cabinet spoke with deep appreciation of the Baptists, although he himself was a Communist. He said that Polish Baptists were a part of Polish history and that the government would continue to grant them full religious liberty to preach and teach as they always had in Poland.

In the plans for rebuilding the city of Warsaw, the government had provided a lot on which the Baptists could build a church and a seminary. Baptists of the world rallied to help make the dream of Polish Baptists come true. Gifts poured in from many lands, and little by little the building began to take shape. Finally, in a glorious service of dedication, it was consecrated to the service of men and the glory of God.

All of this was achieved by a little dedicated band of pastors and people, but the moving spirit in it all was Alexander Kircun. He was born in Wilno, Poland, and was led to Christ by his minister father and was baptized at the age of eighteen. From the time of his conversion he was active in youth groups and later served for a time as president of Polish Baptist Young People. He received his ministerial education at the Baptist

Theological Seminary in Lodz, and also studied in Hamburg, Germany, and Ruschlikon, Switzerland. He was married in 1929, and he and his wife have five children. Their older son plans to follow in his father's footsteps as a Baptist pastor.

Here is what Kircun himself says about his experiences with the Lord:

"I was a sinner and I was born again in my Lord. This change was complete and remains essential for the whole of my life. Many times in my life I have experienced the Lord's presence and help. Three times I went through war and changing fighting lines, though not in the army myself. Amidst all the epidemics and economic and strategic disasters, God spared me. One day a bomb fell just five meters away from a group of people and me. The impact was so strong that it threw us some distance away. The explosion of the bomb did not harm us, because the bomb was not tempered equally and the full force of the explosion went in the direction opposite us. I saw so many wounded and killed about me so often that I could not remain blind to God's providence.

"During the Nazi occupation, many of my colleagues went to the West, but I had an inner conviction not to do so. The West was tempting. It promised better living standards and, so it seemed, more peace and quiet, but my family and I remained admidst the ruins of Warsaw. I never have regretted that decision, for I again experienced God's presence and care many times. It has been a joy to see the growth of a small group of believers from the little band of fourteen that survived the war. Year after year I have seen it grow. Warsaw rose again, and so did the church. The conferences and the visits of our brothers from abroad were a joy and strength to us. Our centennial celebration was also a grand experience. We were simply astounded by our Lord's power as it was shown to us.

"The most moving experience was in the time from 1958 to 1961, when our new church and our Central Baptist Building were being built. Some people said it was 'hitching our wagon to a star,' but having so many evidences of God's help in previous times, I said, 'We shall try.' We trusted our Lord and our Baptist brothers all over the world—and we were not disappointed. Many times we seemed on the verge of failure, when we saw the empty bottom of the cash box, but I knew God was true—and in time our hopes were fulfilled and our dream came true."

Mr. Kircun has traveled in many European countries and in the United States and Canada in the interests of his people and to promote the fellowship of the Baptist World Alliance. He represented Polish Baptists at the Baptist World Congress in Rio de Janeiro, Brazil, in 1960, and also at Miami Beach, where he was elected a vice-president of the Alliance.

It is difficult for those who live in a land where there are many Baptists to understand how much such a world fellowship means to Baptists who are a tiny minority. Those of us who have felt the touch of his spirit have been deeply moved and inspired by the consecration of Alexander Kircun, our brother in Christ. He himself tells how much this larger fellowship means to him:

"I have met Baptist leaders from many lands and admire their dedication, sincerity, brotherhood, progress, and deep understanding. All this I regard as my experience with God in the Lord Jesus Christ to whom I owe so much. I would like to deepen this experience, and particularly I would like to live to see God's greater revelation in evangelism and the extension of his living church."

Russia

Yakov Zhidkov

The beloved, bearded leader of the Baptists of Russia for many years is Yakov Zhidkov. Born in 1885, near what is now Volgograd, he is the second generation of Baptists in his family. His parents were Molokans, a group of believers who drifted away from the Orthodox Church because of their belief in a more personal gospel and in individual salvation through faith. Because of this background, when Baptists moved into the neighborhood, they soon joined with them. After his conversion, Yakov's father distributed Bibles for the British Bible Society.

Yakov Zhidkov was converted when he was about fifteen years of age but was not baptized until he was eighteen. Russian Baptists delay baptism to allow time for instruction and the opportunity for the individual to prove himself worthy of membership in the church family. Yakov became active in youth work and later as a preacher. He went first to Kharkov and then to Leningrad, where he came in touch with other Baptist leaders. When the capital of Russia moved to Moscow in 1931, he went there from Leningrad and soon became chairman of the Evangelical Christian Union.

He was married in 1908 to a very devout Christian. Thirteen

children were born to this union. Three sons died in World War II, and one more died later as a result of the war. Yakov Zhidkov's faith endured through all this sorrow and through all the days of difficulty when Baptists were in disfavor with the government and had to worship in their own homes if at all.

Like many other believers, he endured many hardships for Christ's sake. But when the day of liberation came, Yakov Zhidkov was asked to head the new All-Union Council of Evangelical Christian Baptists, which is the responsible body for Baptist life and work in Russia today.

It was my privilege to travel for many hundreds of miles in Russia with Mr. Zhidkov and others and to visit Baptist churches in Leningrad and Moscow. Down the Ukraine we worshiped and preached in Kiev and Kharkov, Yalta and Odessa, as well as many village churches. Everywhere the people heard their leader with keen interest and deep joy. It was heartening to see the love and respect in which he was held, for they knew he had suffered much for Christ's sake and their hearts were stirred when he preached and prayed.

One Sunday in Moscow, in the only Baptist church allowed in that city of four million people, it was my privilege to share with Yakov Zhidkov in conducting the Lord's Supper.

On the table was a tremendous round loaf of bread Mrs. Zhidkov had baked. As Pastor Zhidkov and I stood together at the Lord's Table, I could not help but think that this was the first time in many years that an American and a Russian had stood together at the Lord's table for such an observance.

In my own heart I thanked God for the privilege and for the faith that had brought us together. After some brief but appropriate words about the symbolism of the bread, Mr. Zhidkov and one of the deacons placed big pieces of bread on the plates which the deacons passed to the crowd of people. Every seat was taken and the aisles were packed. There were even some outside. However, the service moved quietly and reverently, each person breaking off a bit of bread and eating it, bowing in prayer as he did so.

When the bread had been served, I stood at the table and spoke of the symbol of the blood shed for many for the remission of sin. I held in my hands a beautiful silver chalice. It was one of twelve on the table, and I noted that they were not all alike. Later I was told that the different chalices had belonged to a number of Baptist churches that had been required to unite in this one Baptist congregation.

Reverently I took the cup and spoke of its meaning and asked the congregation to join with me in a prayer of thanksgiving for the Christ who loved us and gave himself for us, reminding them that "the blood of Jesus Christ, God's Son, cleanseth us from all sin. This is my blood of the new covenant shed for many for the remission of sin. As often as ye eat this bread and drink this cup ye do proclaim the Lord's death until he comes."

The deacons took the chalices and they were followed by deaconesses, bearing flagons of grape juice so that the cups could be refilled. They were passed from believer to believer and each took a brief sip. One deacon went outside to see that those who could not get in were served with bread and with the cup. The others passed through the congregation until all were served. Then, with deep reverence and with my own heart filled with emotion, we sang the beloved hymn "Blest Be the Tie."

We were still Russian and American as we stood together at

the table, but we were one in Jesus Christ, and in the larger
fellowship of believers that includes Baptists and other Christians in many lands.

One beautiful morning we drove out into the country to
Yakov Zhidkov's home in a village, some miles out from the
city. The village was a typical Russian town with unpaved
streets and small cottages—most of them built of wood. They
nestled under the trees on small lots. A few had larger pieces
of land with garden plots, bearing abundant fruits and vegetables.

The Zhidkovs live in a log house, built on about an acre of
land, with trees in front and a beautiful garden behind. The
logs had been stripped of bark, and the house was well con-
structed. Father and mother shared the small house with two
of their sons and their families, so things were crowded but
comfortable. It was a joy to relax under the trees and to talk
with the other pastors. Some conversed in German, but the
rest of us had an interpreter. We talked informally about life
in Russia, about past experiences, and about the future of our
Baptist work. We wandered around the garden, looking at the
flowers and fresh vegetables and taking pictures.

After a time of fellowship, we were served a bountiful Russian meal on the front porch of the house. Several of the ladies
from the church had come to help Mrs. Zhidkov, but those of
us who sat at the table were the ones who really needed the
help! It was a feast to remember. Each woman had brought
the best she could prepare to add to all that our host and his
family had made ready.

We lingered long at the table singing and talking. There
were toasts and responses and expressions of esteem and
friendship, and we had a chance to see our Russian friends as

we never could have in the crowded city streets or the even more crowded Baptist church.

Something of the spirit of Yakov Zhidkov can be learned from the experience of his son Michael, who is now the third generation of ministers in the Zhidkov family. Michael had grown up in a Christian family and in a Christian church. Family worship and attendance at church were a real part of his life. When he was twelve years old, he was asked if he were a Christian. He said, "Why, yes, of course." However, deep in his heart he was not satisfied. One day a picture of Christ on the cross touched his heart and he became more faithful in his church attendance and joined the choir. One day when a choir member accepted Christ, Michael was deeply moved as he saw a change in the man's face and a new light in his eyes.

Michael began to feel that he too must accept Christ as his personal Saviour. He kept putting it off until one day, while walking home with an aunt, he was deeply moved. "I decided I could wait no longer. I was crossing the street at the moment, and as soon as we reached the other side I asked my aunt to stop and pray with me. Then and there I accepted Christ as Lord and Saviour."

When Michael reached home he told his mother of his experience. Being a very devout woman and one given to much prayer, her reaction was an emotional expression of her faith. But Mr. Zhidkov was calm and, as Michael puts it, almost indifferent. The next morning he said, "Son, I want to talk with you. Religion is a matter not of emotion alone but of responsibility. No one should become a Christian to attain heavenly joy. Rather, he must be faithful and do his duty as a Christian. Then heavenly joy will come."

Michael bears his own testimony to the faith of his father

and his own, as he says, "I was born in Leningrad. I was born again on a street in Moscow."

So, the gospel of Christ goes on, as one soul is lighted by another and each in turn finds the personal faith in Christ as Saviour and Lord that is at the heart of the Christian gospel. It can happen on the streets of Moscow, New York, or any other city in the world. It can happen in a quiet farm home or in the midst of the daily busyness of life. The government may be totalitarian or democratic. The ruling ideology may be Communist or Christian, but the Spirit still speaks to the hearts of men, as he has to three generations of the Zhidkov family. Such a living faith has triumphed in spite of oppression and trial, danger and difficulty. It will continue to win converts as long as men like Yakov Zhidkov find personal, satisfying faith in Christ as Saviour and Lord, and so bear witness to it by word and by deed that their own children and others count it their greatest joy publicly to confess Christ as Saviour and Lord—cost what it may—and to bear their own witness to Christ, the living Lord.

Russia

The Ninety and Nine

He was just a humble Baptist pastor on a great Communist farm in the heart of Russia. I do not even know his name, but I shall not soon forget him. We had driven out into the country because we had told our Russian hosts that we wanted to visit churches in cities and villages and in the open country. We were far more interested in being with Baptist people than in seeing some of the more famous sights usually shown to tourists.

We were in the bounds of a vast farm that included hundreds of acres. It was tilled by many workers who lived as a commune, sharing all things in common. Other farms were tilled for the government, but each farmer had a tiny plot that was his own and he could do with it as he wished. Somehow, the produce on those little private acres seemed far better cared for than anything else. There were several hundred people working on the great farm we were to visit.

We stopped inside a small clearing and saw before us a cottage with a thatched roof. On the roof there was a tiny cross—small but unmistakable—made of two tree branches that had been bound together and placed in the thatch. A crowd had gathered already in expectation of our coming, and the pastor came forward to meet us. He was a simple, quiet man—actually one of the farm workers. He was dressed for the day in his best suit of black, as is the custom for preachers in Russia and many other lands. Warmly he welcomed us to Russia and the farm and to the service of worship.

The congregation met in just one room of the simple cottage. A family lived in the rest of the house, a family of believers. As we walked into the little room, we saw rushes spread on the floor, rude benches of planks with no backs, and a simple pulpit stand. We sat on the bench behind the pulpit as others crowded in until every seat was taken and all the standing room was filled. Others clustered about the windows as the service began. There was singing in a minor key and very slowly, although anyone would have recognized the hymns because of their familiar tunes. The members sang in Russian and we in English. We were one in Christ. One of the ministers led in prayer and the congregation prayed audibly, as is their custom. They listened reverently and often tearfully as the Scripture passage was read and as the gospel was preached. We told them about the Baptists of the world and of the faith that binds us together. I presented the pastor with a Bible in Russian, explaining that I could not read it but I cherished it as much as did he and his congregation. We hoped that after we had gone the Bible would be a living symbol of our fellowship in the living Christ.

After the service, we were served a bounteous farm meal. The menu included bread, fruit, and meat, as one might expect, but there were also Russian borsch and fried goose. When we thought we had eaten all we possibly could, some young girls came running up the hill from a nearby spring where they had kept cool some bowls of delicious sour cream.

The meal and the fellowship were wonderful indeed, and the service had been inspiring. But the most thrilling thing was learning how this church with ninety-nine members came to be on this Communist farm where, presumably, atheism is taught to the children in the schools and there is no real opportunity to witness for the Christian faith?

The pastor is the secret. He was converted at a meeting he attended in a Baptist church in the city. With a Bible in his hand and a heart burning with the desire to win others to his newfound Lord and to the richness of faith that his Christian decision had brought to him, he returned to the farm. One by one, he won others on the farm until now he had ninety-nine who would bear witness to their faith in Christ by being publicly baptized and uniting with the church at the very heart of a great Communist farm.

Here was the opposite of the story Jesus told of the ninety and nine and the one who had gone astray. One had been found and he had won the ninety-nine in the face of almost unbelievable difficulties.

Who could forget such a Christian? Surely, there is rejoicing in the presence of the angels of God over the one plus ninety and nine who have repented.

Russia

The Big Deacon

The "Big Deacon," as we all affectionately and respectfully called him, was the head deacon in a little Baptist church in Russia. After a beautiful and memorable service in the lovely little church in the village where he lived, he invited the pastor and the visitors from overseas and a few of the leaders in the church to come to his home for dinner.

He lived in a stone house, surrounded by a courtyard, with flowers all about. We washed our hands at the pump outside and then were greeted by his wife and daughter and others in the family.

Inside we sat around a big table and ate Russian borsch, black bread, and other distinctive Ukrainian dishes. As we ate, the young people who had been in the choir at the church service stood on one side of the room and sang Ukrainian folk songs and gospel hymns. After the dinner, we expressed appreciation and gratitude to our host and his wife. Then he told us how welcome we were and how glad they were to have us in their home and in their church. Reaching out his hand, he drew his eighteen-year-old daughter out of the choir to stand beside him. "You didn't know when you came that today is our daughter's eighteenth birthday, but you are helping us celebrate that big day in her life." Of course, we all applauded and sang "Happy Birthday," both in English and in Russian.

Then the "Big Deacon" went on. "But, better still, last Sunday our daughter publicly accepted Jesus Christ as her Saviour and asked for membership in the church." Tears filled his eyes, and ours, for we knew how much that meant.

In Russia no one can be accepted into church membership before he reaches eighteen years of age. Even then, applicants are received only after a year or two of training and probation. In the public schools children are taught that there is no God. The deacon's daughter had made her own choice. Church and home had won. We noted the approving glances from others in the youth choir and knew that they, too, would give their lives to Christ and the church, if they had not already done so.

In a land where atheism is taught openly and churches are restricted to worship only within a limited number of buildings, there can be no Sunday School, no Training Union, no youth groups, no social service work. All training of youth is in the hands of the state.

What then brought this daughter to her decision to accept Christ as Saviour and Lord and to commit her life to the Christian cause? The answer is found in the influence of a Christian home, the daily witness of her father and mother, and in the training and teaching that only such a home can give.

Two verses of Scripture, carved on identical wooden plaques hanging on the wall, told the story. Our host explained them with a smile. "Those were our gifts to each other on our wedding day."

We knew then that this had been a Christian home through times of persecution and trial. During all those years when public observance of religion was forbidden in Russia, this family had maintained its faith within its own household and had worshiped in secret until they could do so publicly again. That utter devotion to Christ, in the face of trial and danger, had borne fruit in the decision of the daughter to accept Christ as her Saviour.

Small wonder that, although we met the "Big Deacon" only once for a few hours on a single day, those of us who were there will never forget him. Surely "the righteous shall live by faith," but the faith shall live through the righteous.

Yugoslavia

Franjo Klem

      Franjo Klem's native land of Yugoslavia is Communist, under Marshal Tito. Franjo delights in going to a community where there is no Baptist church, starting one, and getting it to the point where it can continue under a new pastor, while he goes to a new community to start another church in the face of Communist disbelief and opposition.

Franjo was born in Bosanski Brod, in 1916. While still in his teens, his parents moved to Zagreb, where they lived in great poverty. Once a fisherman on the Danube, Franjo's father began to work on the railroad. He liked alcoholic beverages too well but somehow managed for Franjo to finish grammar school and become a barber's apprentice.

In 1934, soon after they went to Zagreb, the Klems were invited to attend a small meeting of Baptists. Traditionally Roman Catholic, Franjo says they didn't know much about the Bible or a genuine Christian life. Telling of his conversion, he says:

"I was then sixteen years of age and it was the first time I had heard anything about the Bible in language I could understand. I became a regular visitor of the Baptist church, but it was two years before I understood clearly about my relationship to God. I had to battle between the world and sinful life, which I loved very much, and the Lord's call for salvation. But, in 1935, Jesus conquered me and I was converted and baptized in the Sava River in Zagreb. Soon after I dedicated my life to Jesus, I learned that it was his will that I serve him as a preacher of the gospel."

Franjo wanted very much to study in one of our Baptist seminaries—either in Bucharest, Romania, or in Hamburg, Germany. His brethren, however, refused to support him in this move, saying that he did not have enough education to go to a theological school. The Baptist people in Yugoslavia at that time believed that pastors and preachers did not need any special training, that they were to speak as they were led of the Holy Spirit. To this very day, many of the pastors in Yugoslavia are lay preachers, some of them very dedicated and zealous students of the Bible.

Unable to go to a seminary, Franjo began to serve with a young Baptist from America, Andrew Derchar, who was supported by a group of businessmen in Los Angeles. Mr. Derchar was born in Yugoslavia but had moved to the United States when he was a boy. When he became a Christian, he wanted to preach the gospel in his native land but needed somone who could speak the language. For about nine months Franjo did mission work in his own country with the young American. Then he had to go into the army, but a small Baptist congregation had been formed before he left.

During this time, the country was occupied by Germans and Italians. Since they were largely Catholic, Baptists suffered a great deal of persecution. Some were put into concentration camps, while others fled to the partisans in the mountains. Andrew Derchar was killed, and Franjo calls him "the first

Baptist martyr in Yugoslavia." Later Franjo himself was captured and put into a prison camp in Germany, but after three
months was allowed to go home.

John Allen Moore, a Southern Baptist missionary, had spent
several years in Yugoslavia. When he learned that Franjo was
free, he invited him to study at the Baptist seminary in Buda-
pest, Hungary. Franjo gladly accepted but was dismayed when
he found that it would take seven years to do the necessary
preparatory work and finish the seminary. This was more time
than he felt he could allow. So, remembering the words of
Matthew 19:26, "With God all things are possible," he determined to finish the work in three years. It was a hard and trying
time but he reached his goal, only to be told by the Hungarian
police the very day he graduated that he must leave the country
in twenty-four hours. Then he realized why the Lord had
helped him complete the work so rapidly.

Franjo returned to Zagreb and again took up his pastorate,
until he was drafted into service by the Fascist Croatian Army,
as a meteorologist. Since he was stationed in Zagreb, he could
continue serving as pastor of the church, which by that time was
compelled to meet in secret. Public worship was forbidden and
the sanctuary was being used as a German military depot.

When the partisans, under Tito, finally brought liberation,
Franjo was sent to a prison camp for a few weeks. He was released when Tito signed an amnesty and all political prisoners
were set free. All the Baptist churches in Yugoslavia were told
they once again were free to worship publicly, and Franjo continued as pastor of the Zagreb church.

During this time of stress and strain, he married a lovely
Christian girl. The Lord soon gave them a son to whom they
gave the name of Velimir, which means "grand peace." Three

years later they were blessed with another son whom they called Theodor, "the gift of God." After this, when the doctor informed them that Mrs. Klem should not have more children, they adopted a ten-year-old girl who lived in their home until she married a fine young Christian businessman. Some years later, much to their delight, Mrs. Klem gave birth to two lovely girls, Mary and Martha. In spite of the doctor's fears, they were born safely and well on Mother's Day. What a lovely Mother's Day gift! As Franjo says, "Once more we experienced how wonderful our Lord is!"

From Zagreb, Franjo and his family moved to Daruvar, which was the center of an old Baptist mission started in the 1880s. He was pastor of all six churches in the association and served ten mission stations in addition. It was a hard and difficult field because the churches were in a radius of about sixty miles and the only practical means of transportation was bicycle. To reach some stations, he even had to leave the bicycle and go on foot. When Franjo went to Daruvar there was no church building, but before long there was a lovely Baptist chapel which was called Bethania. The membership in the association more than doubled in the next few years.

With the work at Daruvar in good condition, Franjo moved on to Sisak where three Baptist families were trying to organize a Baptist church. Franjo had just made his first visit to the United States, where he studied Sunday School work. So his work in Sisak began with something new to Yugoslavia, an "all-age" Sunday School. Up to that time Sunday School was for children up to fourteen years of age. In a short time the church had over forty members and the work grew and prospered.

Then it was time for Franjo to move on. He and his family

went to Rijeka, a port city with about one hundred thousand inhabitants, and proceeded to organize a Baptist church there. They started with five members—all of them boys. The big problem was a meeting place. The only one they could find was twenty steps underground, with no ventilation. Because this was so unsatisfactory and people would not come, the Klems arranged two bedrooms in their home for a chapel, which seated seventy people. The family was pressed into one small bedroom with the boys sleeping in a closet. But, as the Klems said, "We had a regular place to meet and glorify our Lord Jesus Christ." Today, there are forty-two members—80 percent of them young people.

Franjo has also been a leader in organizing the Baptist Union in Yugoslavia and was its secretary for a number of years. He helped to start literature work and took the lead in printing their first songbook. He helped develop a handbook for Sunday School teachers and a guide for daily worship. He also organized the youth work and helped to hold the first Youth Congress in Yugoslavia in 1955.

One of the primary needs in Yugoslavia was a theological seminary. Finally, in 1953, Franjo and others were able to start one. For two years classes met in their apartment in Daruvar, but, finally, the seminary was established in a nice building in Novi Sad.

In 1960, en route to Rio de Janeiro for the Baptist World Congress, Franjo again visited the Baptist Sunday School Board in Nashville, Tennessee, and spent about four months visiting Baptist churches in twenty-three states.

He tells of one experience he had in Birmingham, Alabama. In the middle of the racial crisis, he boarded a bus for another city. The only empty seat was next to a Negro woman. He heard a slight rumble of discussion but sat quietly, not sure just what it was all about. Finally a white woman turned to him and said, "You have no business sitting there." A young man from the front of the bus came back and told Franjo he should move. Seeing no place to move, Franjo kept his seat. Finally, the bus driver came aboard. Sensing the situation, he announced, "The young white man seated toward the rear of the bus is a Baptist minister from Yugoslavia. He is just a visitor to our country."

The murmuring stopped abruptly. The Negro woman with whom he was sitting held out her hand, smiled, and said, "I am a Baptist too." The white woman who had rebuked him turned and said, "Excuse me, I am sorry I spoke to you as I did. I too am a Baptist." The young man from the front came back and apologized, explaining that he also was a Baptist and held out his hand in friendship. They rode for several miles singing Christian hymns together. A completely new spirit was evident.

Baptists in Yugoslavia still suffer many difficulties and restrictions, but the work goes on. The only time they can preach outside of their churches is at a burial service. Franjo smiled as he told me of the time he conducted the funeral of a well-known man. A big crowd gathered and Franjo took advantage of the opportunity—preaching for nearly an hour as he stood by the open grave! When the service finally ended, the policeman assigned to guard the proceedings said with a grin, "I think you Baptists are even glad when somebody dies, because it gives you a chance to preach the gospel."

Franjo Klem is a good servant of Jesus Christ, and a courageous one as well. There are many others like him in Yugoslavia, and the witness for Christ goes on.

A Farmer

After a long and dusty journey by car, we finally reached our destination in a Communist land in eastern Europe. We went to the stone house of the leading deacon of the Baptist church and found that he and his wife were waiting for us. They invited us in and gave us refreshments. Their home was simply furnished. On the stand by the bed was a Bible, worn from constant use. We walked through the room that served as kitchen and dining room into a guest room. On the wall was a picture of Billy Graham. As I spoke of my surprise, our host said: "We hear him sometimes on the radio and we read about him. He is surely God's man and we hope some day he can visit us here."

We asked about the service in the church at which we were expected to preach.

"Oh, it is already under way." The deacon explained that the service had begun at four, but that we would be in plenty of time for our part. Two of us were expected to preach, but others had already been leading the worship and preaching for over an hour before we arrived. We walked slowly through the village streets, intrigued by the thatched-roof stone houses and the walled-in courtyards where every farmer kept his cattle.

When we reached the church, we were greeted outside by a group of children and young people. Inside, the men were seated on one side, the women on the other. One of the deacons had just finished preaching and the choir was preparing to sing.

After some beautiful and spirited music, Robert Denny, associate secretary of the Baptist World Alliance, told about our Baptist World Fellowship. His message was interpreted by one of the national pastors who had come with us. Then I spoke, through our interpreter, on "The Faith That Makes Us One in Jesus Christ."

When I finished speaking, I expected the benediction. One deacon looked at the other and said, "It's too early to go home." The other agreed, and so after some music by the choir, they asked each of the two national pastors who came with us to preach.

After the service, we made our way, through the darkness, back to the home of the deacon. As we went in and sat down with the farmer and his brother, we were served soup and wonderful homemade bread and a simple meal by his good wife. The young people stayed in the courtyard, singing hymn after hymn as we ate.

On the porch were stacked bags of grain. The farmer explained that the rulers of the land would take the grain when they were ready and at their own price. He told of the many restrictions and difficulties Baptist farmers faced.

Finally, I asked, "How will you endure all this?"

In one mute but eloquent gesture, he simply lifted his hand and pointed to the sky, and we understood. He could say, as did his Master of old: "I am not alone; the Father is with me."

And we could say as we sat there and as we left, "Surely the Lord is in this place."

A Christian Homemaker

A woman, who must go unnamed, recently visited one of the "free countries" of Europe. Coming from one of the most oppressed nations in eastern Europe, she had to come alone, leaving behind her husband and family as assurance of her return.

When friends learned of the difficulties and hardships she and her family were facing as Christians, they said, "Tell us what you want most to take back with you and we shall be happy to get it for you."

To their amazement she replied, "I want just three things: a new Bible in my own language, a Bible in German for a friend, and two theological books for my husband." In amazement, her friends asked, "Do you want nothing else?"

"Nothing," she said, "these are far more important than anything else I could take."

Truly, God's Word is to her the Bread of life. She knows what it means to say, "Thy word is a lamp unto my feet, and a light unto my path."

Faith and Courage

J. H. Rushbrooke, for many years secretary and, finally, president of the Baptist World Alliance, loved to tell stories illustrating the faith and courage of Baptists in many lands. When he and George W. Truett came back from a journey in eastern Europe, they both spoke with deep feeling about one young Baptist leader in a Communist land who, with a gaunt face but shining eyes, said to them after an inspiring meeting: "Sirs, we shall probably never meet again in this world. We shall face many hardships and difficulties after you have gone, but I want you to know one thing—that no matter what happens, we shall be true and we shall keep faith. Although you may not see us nor hear from us, you can count on that."

Baptist work in that land has prospered, in spite of difficulties and opposition. Many heroes and heroines of our faith are nameless, but God's work goes on, because they keep the faith.

One Baptist layman, a business leader in his community, whose little land was overrun by invaders quietly joined the underground movement. Knowing that some day the soldiers or secret police would come to seize him, he asked the Lord to give him wisdom to deal with the situation when it came.

One rainy day he saw a police car come slowly past his house, then go to the rear. He knew that this was the hour. He was thankful that he happened to be alone at the time. When the police surrounded the house and came to the front door, they found a man standing there wearing his hat and raincoat, for it was raining very hard. He was furiously and impatiently ringing the bell. The leader of the police asked, "What is the matter? Is no one here?"

"I have been ringing the bell but I get no response."

Again the policeman asked, "What are you doing here?"

"I want to get my vacuum cleaner that these people have been using."

The policeman said, "Well, we are going in," and he ordered his men to break in the door. As they went in and the officer sent his men to search the house, the man in the raincoat said quietly, "That's my vacuum cleaner standing there in the hall. Do you mind if I take it?"

The police captain said, "Why no, if it's yours take it and go along. We don't want it."

And so the Christian layman walked away from his own house with his own vacuum cleaner under his arm, made his escape, and later safely got away with his family.

In a more serious tone, Dr. Rushbrooke would tell of another pastor in an invaded land. The officers in charge called him up twenty-five times for questioning. They wanted to know the members of his congregation and all the facts about them. They were interested in any information he could give about those who might be betraying the invaders or plotting against them. The pastor steadfastly refused to give any information about his congregation or friends.

The twenty-sixth time the officer was much firmer and far

more threatening than before. He said, "In the past we have been patient with you, but we are losing our patience. You must tell us the information we want, or we shall arrest you and take you away from your congregation and charge you with failure to cooperate."

The pastor steadfastly refused, saying, "As I have told you before, I will not betray my people. God helping me, I will keep quiet."

The officer replied, "God can't help you now. You are in our hands." With the warning that the next time they would expect better cooperation, they finally let him go once more.

God did help this pastor and his congregation. Secretly and quietly, they were carried by boats from the shores of their native land to safety in another country by Christians who did the same service for many refugees and a number of beleaguered little congregations. The pastor and his people still live on, worshiping God and serving the Lord Christ in a new land. They know the poet Browning's words are true:

> Our times are in His hand who says, "A whole I planned.
> Trust God—see all—nor be afraid."

LATIN AMERICA

Argentina

Alfonso Olmedo

A thirty-day voyage from Buenos Aires on a Norwegian ship being sought by the German Navy during World War II brought Alfonso Olmedo to New Orleans to study in what is now New Orleans Baptist Theological Seminary. The ship had disobeyed orders to call in German-controlled ports, and the German Navy had been ordered to destroy it. Two trips later it was sunk with no survivors.

Alfonso was born in 1915 on a big ranch in the state of Córdoba in the interior of Argentina. Several of his relatives are either nuns or priests of the Roman Catholic Church. His older sister is the superior of an order of nuns, devoted to serving the poor and the working class in Argentina.

When Alfonso was four, the family moved to the city of Rosario, the second largest city in Argentina. "There," Alfonso says, "I was born again in August of 1935, while attending a night course of six years in business college." A devout, practicing Catholic, Alfonso thought he could win to his religion a classmate who was a member of the First Baptist Church of Rosario. After sixteen months of argument and struggle, the Baptist won instead, and Alfonso surrendered to Christ and began to attend the Baptist church whenever possible. For two

73

years he underwent severe persecution and was able to attend church only about ten times in the two years. In August, 1937, however, he applied for baptism and became a member of the First Baptist Church.

Shortly after this the family moved to Buenos Aires, where he joined the Caballito Baptist Church. His father became ill and passed away, and the support of the family, then in very difficult circumstances, fell upon Alfonso. Only one of the brothers had a job and he soon lost that because of political differences.

One day when Alfonso was not at home a rich lady, who owned a ranch near his birthplace, came to offer him a job as bookkeeper. As soon as he came home his family told him about the job, warning him not to refuse it. He tells the story:

"I went to see her. Very kindly she told me I was not supposed to say one word about my religion while I worked for her, for all her people and ranch tenants were Roman Catholics. I struggled long trying to soften her conditions, and, finally, unable to, but thinking that even if I did not say a word for Christ I could so live before them that I could win them with my life, I accepted and left.

"Riding the subway on the way back, the Spirit of the Lord spoke to me, telling me I had done wrong. Again a struggle, until I left the subway midway from home, went to a telephone and phoned her, telling her I was sorry I had promised that I would take the job. I could not but speak for him who had done such great things unto me and I could not take a job with such a prohibition. The lady was stunned. She cried, 'I congratulate you, Alfonso! God bless you! He must help you.'

"Back home I was greeted by a chorus as soon as I entered the door. Mother, grandmother, brothers, and sisters, all at once, 'Did you accept?' When I told them the outcome—what a scene! How painful it was to hear their cries and bitter remonstrances—that I did not care for my orphaned little brothers, that I did not love my widowed mother, etc. Somehow, it came upon me that the Lord would not let me down when I was suffering such shame for his sake, that he must help. Without knowing how, I told them, 'Do not worry, please. Next week I shall have a job here in Buenos Aires.' They laughed at me in scorn. It was impossible at that time, even for the people with friends, to find a job. How could I, a poor nobody, a poor 'evangelical,' get a job?

"About the middle of the following week, I was walking down Buenos Aires' fashionable Florida Street. I saw a beautiful tall building with a sign *BANCO POPULAR ARGENTINO*. I went in, asked for a job, took a test, was recommended by a friend inside (a member of the church I was attending), and that Saturday an employee of the bank knocked at the door of my home to tell me I was employed! No words could tell what that meant to my family. I stayed in that bank until leaving for New Orleans."

While working in the bank, Olmedo learned that "the service of Jesus true pleasure affords." He greatly enjoyed his church, where he served as president of the Young People's Union, Sunday School superintendent, and teacher. Soon he became president of the Sunday School of the Buenos Aires Association and a leader in youth work in the city. Whenever there was an opportunity, he preached in churches, tents, public squares, and street corners in and around Buenos Aires.

"Finally in 1941," says Olmedo, "I heard the the voice of Jesus saying, 'Whom shall I send, and who will go for us?' I answered, 'Here I am, Lord, send me!' Somehow it had become

my conviction I should go to the Belgian Congo as a missionary.
The Lord had done such marvelous things in my conversion
and my preservation through dangerous persecution, I felt I
should do the hardest for him. With that in my mind and heart,
on July 21, 1941, I resigned my banking position and left for
Baptist Bible Institute in New Orleans, sailing the seas for thirty
days from Buenos Aires to Boston aboard a Norwegian ship,
the S. S. *Tabor*. They gave me a job to pay my way. I washed
dishes, shined brass, and mopped decks. How joyfully I used to
sing:

> *Vivir por Cristo será mi afan*
> *lo que le plazca mis manos harán!*

(This is a free translation of 'Living for Jesus wherever I am,
doing each duty in his holy name.' But in Spanish it says literally, 'That which pleases him, my hands shall perform'—even
washing dishes!) I arrived in New Orleans with thirty-five
cents in my pockets, but a million in my soul."

With the aid of a mission scholarship and work in south
Louisiana, under the state and home mission boards, Alfonso
managed to finance his education. In 1943, he had the joy of
leading in the organization of the first non-Catholic Church in
St. Bernard Parish and became its first pastor. That summer
his sweetheart for five years arrived from Argentina and the
two were married in the Central Baptist Church in Miami by
Dr. C. Roy Angell. Two boys were born to them while they
were in New Orleans. The second died soon after birth, but the
older son is following in his father's footsteps in the Lord's
service.

In the spring of 1945, Olmedo graduated and with his wife
and son sailed for Argentina. The Lord had changed his con-

viction about his place of service and he felt led to go back to
his homeland to preach. He says, "I was as blessed as Jacob—a
wonderful wife, a son, fourteen boxes of books and clothes, and
one thousand dollars in cash as compared with the thirty-five
cents when I arrived." The money came largely from a book
titled *From Darkness Unto Light*, which he wrote about the
story of his conversion.

The First Baptist Church of Austin, Texas, sponsor him as
their missionary, giving both financial and prayer support. He
began his work in the state of San Luis, five hundred miles from
Buenos Aires. Two years later, with ten converts, he organized
the first and only church in a state the size of South Carolina,
though less populated. Growth is slow in Argentina, but the
membership now is nearing one hundred and is sponsoring
three missions.

Alfonso has served four years as president of the Argentine
Baptist Convention and for fifteen years has been on the Execu-
tive Committee and other boards. He has written much for their
national magazine, and represented Argentine Baptists at the
Baptist World congresses in Cleveland, Rio de Janeiro, and
Miami Beach. From 1955 to 1960, he served on the Baptist
World Alliance Executive Committee and was elected a vice-
president in 1960.

Evangelism is his great delight. He has traveled widely,
speaking in seven Latin American countries and in Spain and
conducting evangelistic meetings. Some idea of the effective-
ness of his service can be gained from the words of W. R. White
in the book *That the World May Know*, published by Broadman
in 1947:

Preaching is very effective on mission fields. Among native Christians many strong preachers have been developed. We are thinking

of two very successful revivals that have been conducted recently. One was led by a native preacher of Argentina in a campaign in Chile. The other was directed by one of our missionaries in China. Alfonso Olmedo, one of our native missionaries, was trained in our Seminary at New Orleans. He was invited in the fall of 1946 to conduct a revival in our Colegio Bautista in Temuco, Chile. He is a native of Argentina. According to missionary R. Cecil Moore, he captivated everyone with his preaching. He speaks Spanish, not only correctly, but in a beautiful, attractive style. His deep fervor and heart power remind one of the immortal Dr. Truett. Eight hundred people were crowded into an auditorium which is supposed to seat four hundred. More than a hundred gave their hearts to the Lord.

A serious automobile accident almost took his life and involved him in litigation that might have ruined his career. When the case was tried, he was released when it was obvious to all in the courtroom that the other man involved was lying, and the prosecuting attorney asked that Olmedo be acquitted. Telling of that experience, Alfonso says, "I can remember when I first woke up in the hospital bed and I saw myself in such bad shape—how I wished I had died and gone to be with Christ rather than to live on, not knowing how I would be at the end physically. Yet, soon the Lord changed my outlook, and I began to repeat within my heart, 'I shall not die, but I shall live and praise the Lord'—and it came to pass—praise the Lord!"

Surely it was in the providence of God that Olmedo made the journey safely through dangerous seas in wartime to New Orleans. Hundreds who have been won to Christ through his ministry would join with him in saying, "Praise the Lord!"

Brazil

David Gomes

David Gomes is secretary of the Home Mission Board of the Brazilian Baptist Convention in Rio de Janeiro. Also a popular radio preacher, he is on the air regularly. He has written two books, based on radio listeners' questions and the answers he has given over the air. He is a winsome and effective preacher of the gospel and a radiant and friendly spirit. The love of God is evident day after day to all who know this remarkable man and his wife and seven children.

When I asked David to tell me his story, he said, "I hope I can write something to bring glory to the Christ I love and who saved my soul when I was twelve years old. I am so glad you asked me because it is my first attempt to think through the story of my own life." Here is his story:

The last days of December, 1919, were a time of hardship and great anticipation for the family of railroader Joseph Gomes. Levi, a strong, healthy boy had recently died of diphtheria. Christmas was going to be a sad time for the Gomes family. Mr. Gomes had to leave for work, which was about 175 miles from home. Mrs. Gomes was expecting her eleventh child and the family was eager for the new arrival.

At noon on December 23, 1919, in the town of Itaúna, a small industrial center sixty miles from Belo Horizonte, the capital of the state of Minas Gerais, a boy was born to the Gomes family. The father, upon receiving the news by telegram, hurried home to see his new son and named him David.

In that moment of happiness, the father remembered Levi. With a feeling of remorse and to the surprise of his wife, he said, "God doesn't always know what he is doing. Look! Levi was a full-grown boy and a joy to our home. Now with this new boy, we don't even know what he will be like."

The mother, without hesitation, said, "Honey, you're not thinking of what you're saying. Who are we to judge God?"

David's father told him this a short time before his death. He asked for David's forgiveness and at the same time expressed his gratitude to the Lord for his life and for his being the only minister in the family.

Many years later an old friend of the family told David of a promise that his mother had made which she had never told him. He began by citing Jeremiah 1:5, then said:

You can say, as Jeremiah or as Paul, that you belonged to God and his cause before you were born. Your family at that time had recently become Christians. Your mother had been a member of the Woman's Missionary Society and had contributed much in giving of her time and money. Because of her conversion, the Catholics were persecuting her. Your father was being persecuted in his work and the family was suffering hardships because of the decision. . . . During this time, your mother was expecting her eleventh child. Her faith in the Lord had not weakened. When I visited her, she said, "Brother Florentino, pray for me. I want with all my heart that this child might be used by God to bring light and salvation to the lost people in this country."

David writes: "My father's salary was small and, to make ends meet, everyone in the family worked. My older sisters worked in a fabric factory and the smaller children went with Mother to look for firewood. She bundled it for us to carry home. We sang hymns as we cut the wood and Mother bundled it. When I was just six I would carry my father's lunch to him. He was working as a blacksmith about three-fourths of a mile from the center of town. As he ate lunch, I would work the bellows to help him shape the iron.

"We bought milk and Mother made cakes, cookies, and candies. It was my responsibility to sell them. I always had good luck with selling and had some regular customers. Sometimes I helped an older brother sell newspapers. We didn't make much, but it helped to meet our needs.

"Sundays were always special for us. Everyone put on his best clothes and off to church we would go. I remember one Sunday in particular when I cried during a sermon. The preacher, H. E. Cockell, spoke on the sin of David. I thought he was talking about me. At a certain point the preacher said, "After being reprimanded by Nathan, there wasn't anything David could do; he went to his bedroom and cried." At that time someone cried and cried—it was another David!

"My father was transferred to Belo Horizonte to be in charge of a warehouse. It was a big promotion. . . .

"I enrolled in grade school, where I had many enriching experiences. One of them I have used many times in my sermons. Each Thursday the priest from the Catholic Church taught catechism at school. The non-Catholics were not required to attend these classes as there is, supposedly, separation of church and state in Brazil. Therefore, there is individual liberty. My parents told me to leave the room when the priest arrived. I remember how disappointed I was the first time the priest came. I arose to leave, thinking that the others would do the same.

I was really surprised when I discovered that I was the only person in the group who wasn't a Catholic! This began to disturb me. Was I the only person with the right beliefs and the others were all wrong? This upset me for a long time. My mother told me that I was right and I should leave the rest up to the Lord. This helped, but I didn't feel completely right until one day on the school ground, during recess, I asked my teacher if all my friends were wrong and I was the only right one. She smiled and said, 'There are a lot of Christians in the world. I am a Christian myself and my husband is a pastor.' I can't describe how happy I felt when she told me she was a Christian. I thought, If my teacher is a Christian then I am in the majority. I never felt better in being a Christian than I did at that moment.

"Every day before I left for school my mother would have prayer with me. I would try to leave for school without her seeing me, but as mothers do, she always saw me and brought me back into the house. She would always say, 'The world is big, my son, and we can't face it without God.' Then after prayer I would leave for school.

"My mother was the strong one in the family. She didn't let herself become weighted down with problems. She knew that problems would pass and the best thing to do was to make the best of them. For several months Mother wasn't well. The family doctor was called, but even with the treatment he prescribed nothing seemed to help. The pains continued and death came quickly. I lost my mother when I needed her most. But all through my life I have been strengthened and inspired by her strong and victorious faith, even in the face of affliction and death.

"The first time that I felt a need of Christ was when I heard one of my sisters talking to my oldest brother about his urgent need to accept Christ as his Saviour or he would be lost. Being a son of Christians didn't save him. I listened to the conversation from a distance and became very disturbed about my own relationship with the Lord. I thought, If he is lost then I am too, for we do the same things.

"Time passed. One summer Sunday, on January 26, 1931, when Missionary O. P. Maddox was preaching, I made my decision to accept Christ as my Saviour. After my conversion experience, doors began to open for me. With only a grade-school education, I was limited. However, God had great plans for me.

"On June 19, 1935, in the Barro Preto Baptist Church in Belo Horizonte there was an unforgettable service. Missionary L. M. Bratcher, the corresponding secretary-treasurer of the Home Mission Board spoke. Just a few days before, a layman had spoken in a prayer meeting about the needs in the interior of Brazil and I had been very impressed with what he said. As Dr. Bratcher preached, twenty-five young people felt the call to missions. I was among them. Soon we organized a Life Service Band, composed of those who had recently made a decision.

"After deciding to enter the ministry, the problem of education arose. Before I could gain entrance into high school I had to study some more, and I couldn't depend on my father to help me. Dr. and Mrs. Maddox arranged for a deacon in the First Baptist Church in Belo Horizonte to pay the expenses of my study for the rest of the year. I finished the year with high grades. The next year, Miss Ray Buster, a Southern Baptist missionary and my Sunday School teacher, offered to pay the tuition for my first year of high school and arranged for someone in the United States to help with later expenses. I had to borrow a suit to have my picture made to send to this person. I didn't hear any more about the picture until 1958, when I was returning from the Baptist World Youth Congress in Toronto, Canada. I was entertained by the Lydia Class of the Central Baptist Church, Clovis, New Mexico. I learned that the money for my education had been given by a Mr. Robert Stone and the Lydia Sunday School Class. While I was in Clovis, I was shown the picture that had been taken many years before.

"To pay for the rest of my education I secured a job as a janitor and disciplinarian. I cleaned all the classrooms and helped with the discipline in the dormitory. This took care of my board.

"In 1938, I was elected president of the Young People's Training Union. I didn't know how to preside and I didn't want to accept the office. Through the counsel of some friends, I realized that I would be losing a great privilege if I didn't accept. I accepted it and promised myself that I would never turn down a responsibility that was offered to me. I have fulfilled that promise.

"In 1939, Frank Leavell came to Brazil to organize Baptist student work in the Baptist schools. I was elected president of the BSU Dr. Leavell congratulated me with a big Brazilian-type hug and said that he would do his best to help me. As a result of that work, a preaching point was opened up in the Baptist school. Mrs. Rosalee Appleby, Southern Baptist missionary, was elected counselor. We were blessed in a great way. I preached and Mrs. Appleby made visits. Many souls were won to the Lord. Through this experience, my vision of the work was enlarged. It wasn't long before the Floresta Baptist Church was organized from that preaching point directed by the Baptist students.

"In my third year at the Seminary, Missionary J. J. Cowsert invited me to work in the Publicity Department of the Publishing House. At that time Mr. Cowsert was pastor of the Thomas Coelho Baptist Church. I was called as copastor of that church in 1944, when I graduated from the Seminary, and I was ordained into the ministry on December 1, 1944.

"On November 24, 1944, the Seminary was having its end-of-the-term party, which was really a farewell party to the graduates. Several of the fellows commented about a certain girl who was graduating from the Baptist Girls' School in Rio and who was going to represent her class in the graduation exercises. I was also going to be the speaker for my graduation class. I decided that night to meet her, and as we stood in line for refreshments I made my way to stand beside her. After talking with her for five minutes, I asked her if she would marry me. I scared her, but she didn't say yes or no. On December 23, we became engaged, and on August 11, the following year, we were married in Curitiba, Parana.

"My wife, Haydee Suman, was converted at the age of seventeen through the influence of Missionary Mrs. A. Ben Oliver. Haydee's mother was born in Italy. Several of her brothers and her father were Presbyterians. Haydee was the only Baptist in the family. God had kept her to be my wife.

"We now have seven children: Ana Maria, 14; Priscila, 12; Marcos David, 10; Sophia Regina, 8; Esther Ruth, 6; and Elizabeth, 2. The four oldest are already Christians. Sophia accepted the Lord when she was just seven years old.

"Before we were married we received a letter from a missionary who was on furlough in the U. S. A., saying that we should come to the States to study if we felt it was the Lord's will. We began to pray. The war was on and it was difficult to get tickets. More than once Missionary J. J. Cowsert told me to make our reservations with the Delta Ship Line. I didn't do it though.

"Mrs. Appleby continued making the arrangements in the U. S. A. Women from Yazoo County, Mississippi, arranged for a scholarship. E. D. Head, president of Southwestern Seminary, arranged a job for me at the Seminary. It seemed everything was working out right until the day I went to the Delta office to buy our passages the first part of December. I was told that there were no tickets available and that we would have to wait seven months. Mr. Cowsert took advantage of this and said, 'Didn't I tell you to make your reservations ahead of time!' My only answer was, 'If I'm not supposed to go, I don't want to. If it is God's will, a door will open.' I returned home as if I had never thought about going to the States. The next week I received word from Delta saying that there had been a cancellation and if my wife and I could embark the next day there would be a stateroom available. I immediately sent word that we could sail on the short notice. We only had ten thousand cruzeiros and there wasn't time to borrow more. God answered our prayers, for it was a cargo ship and the passage only cost ten thousand cruzeiros.

"We made our new home at Southwestern Seminary. I worked hard cleaning the dormitories and serving in the dining room for fifty cents an hour. I preached in many churches and made many friends. I bought a lot of used books and studied as much as possible. I received the master of religious education degree and studied other courses also.

"As I look back to those two years in the States, I feel that God was really with us. Many lives touched ours and through them we were enriched. For this and many other reasons we say, and we repeat, that God was in that trip, as he was in our poverty-stricken childhood, in our pastoring experiences, and, above all, in the work that he has for us to do.

"While I was in the States, I received an invitation to pastor the Tijuca Baptist Church in Rio de Janeiro. There were many difficulties, but there were always many more blessings. Dr. and Mrs. A. R. Crabtree, with their captivating personalities marked by love and humility, had left their imprint in the church. There was a happy atmosphere in the church.

"The church agreed to let me have two months a year to hold revivals. I had a month's vacation, so in all I had three months to serve other churches. Invitations began to come from all over Brazil.

"On January 1, 1953, the church began a five-minute program on a small radio station one time a week. I felt that a short commentary should be given on the Sunday School lesson, for the following day was Sunday. Letters of approval began to come in. One person sent five cruzeiros to help support the program. The church realized the need to lengthen the program to ten minutes. Several months later it was decided to include a special word to the Extension Department who listened to the program. Then someone said, 'Our program will be like a school.' The idea had come from God. Today the Bible School of the Air reaches twenty-five thousand students in all parts of Brazil on two shortwave stations and one fifty thousand-watt station. Besides this program of national scope, every day of the year the Bible School of the Air has other programs on local stations and also has correspondence courses."

This, in brief, is the story of David's life thus far, but it is only the beginning. As executive secretary of Brazilian Baptists'

Home Mission Board, he has traveled all over the country, spending at least half of each month in the field, in addition to his radio and publishing ministry. His heart is literally on fire to win others for Christ. Much of the growth in missionary and evangelistic activity in Baptist work in Brazil in recent years is due to his great heart and zealous spirit.

When Baker James Cauthen, executive secretary of the Foreign Mission Board of Southern Baptists, preached the Congress sermon, at the Tenth Baptist World Congress held in Rio de Janeiro, in 1960, David Gomes was his interpreter. It was hard to tell who was preaching and who was interpreting, for they were two men with one mind and heart as they proclaimed God's message for that hour.

Whether on horseback in the interior or on a jet airliner at home or in a distant land, a hymn that has given David confidence and strength is one that has blessed many through the years:

> Lord, I would clasp Thy hand in mine,
> Nor ever murmur nor repine,
> Content, whatever lot I see,
> Since 'tis Thy hand that leadeth me!

Haiti

A Pastor

Early one Sunday morning, Pastor Kelly, the American Baptist missionary in Cap-Haïtien, Haiti, took me to the village of Limbe to preach in the First Baptist Church. As we drove into Limbe, we met the pastor of the Limbe church, a very fine and dedicated young man, as he led his congregation from the church to the river about a mile away. The choir followed him singing gospel songs.

When we reached the river, one by one the candidates publicly confessed their faith in Christ as Saviour and Lord and were buried with him in baptism and raised to walk in newness of life.

When the service ended, the procession returned to the church for a beautiful service of worship.

A lovely Haitian girl read in French an address of welcome to me. I could understand only the word "papa." The pastor interpreted for me, indicating with a smile that she was saying that the Roman Catholics in Limbe had a pope who lived in Rome, Italy. She said, "We Baptists also have a pope who lives in Richmond, Virginia. We know that the Roman Catholic pope would never come to Limbe, but our pope has and we welcome him today."

89

Later on it was my privilege to voice appreciation for the words of welcome. I then tried to explain the difference between a Roman Catholic pope and the president of the Baptist World Alliance! This gave me an opportunity to talk about our Baptist World Fellowship and then to preach about the faith we all share. Although we are of many nations and colors and cultures, we are one in Christ.

After dinner with the pastor and his wife, I watched a few men in the village square tending the cocoa beans spread out to dry in the sun.

Suddenly I was intrigued by a procession coming down a side street and moving across the square. Men were bearing a coffin on their shoulders, and a few others were following behind—most of them with bottles in their hands.

The pastor explained what was going on: "These people are not believers. They called in the witch doctor for his special rites, but the man died. They want no pastor or priest, but are on their way to bury their friend, and then they will drown their sorrows with the bottles in their hands."

The two processions I saw that day speak in sharp contrast of the choice every individual in the world must make.

Those in one procession were without God, without Christ, without hope. They could only hopelessly lay their dead away and then seek to forget their sorrow and grief for the moment, knowing full well that all too soon they too would die and be buried in the same way.

Those in the other procession were believers in a living Christ. They went back to their church and then to their homes with joy in their hearts. They share the faith of all Christians, that in Christ life is ever lord of death, and love shall never lose its own.

Jamaica

J. A. Leo-Rhynie

At the end of nearly a century and a half, a native Jamaican was called for the first time as pastor of the famous East Queen Street Baptist Church in Kingston, Jamaica. That man was J. A. Leo-Rhynie, who gives as the text of his life, "I am debtor" (Rom. 1:14).

Why was this man chosen and how did he happen to be ready when the time came for one of his own race to be pastor of this historic and influential Baptist church, the largest in all the Caribbean? Let Leo-Rhynie tell it in his own words:

"One event in my life which left an indelible imprint on my mind and intensified the inner constraint to live all my life in the service of Christ and mankind was my deliverance from drowning in a river. My companions, in panic, fled the scene and gave me up as lost. I was then about fourteen years of age. I cannot explain all that happened, but that morning a strong hand raised me from the 'blue hole' of the river and literally pushed me onto a rock. When I came to myself I saw no one. I thanked God for my deliverance and applied the words of the psalmist to my experience: 'He brought me up out of the horrible pit, out of the miry bog, and set my feet upon a rock, steadying my steps, and established my goings.' While the news of my 'drowning' was being noised abroad, I walked with God along my beaten track three miles back home, saying all along, 'Hitherto hath the Lord helped me, henceforth I will serve Him.' "

Leo-Rhynie was born at Salt Springs, three miles from Montego Bay, in the parish of Saint James in beautiful Jamaica, in June, 1908. His parents were among the leading citizens of the community and devoted Christians. Joscelyn was the youngest of their five children. He gave his heart to the Lord when he was only five years of age and grew up giving every promise of being a preacher of the gospel. After attending primary school and high school, at the early age of eighteen he entered Calabar Theological Seminary, founded many years ago by British Baptists, to prepare for the Christian ministry.

While in seminary, he had another bitter experience that might well have turned him aside from the ministry. After spending three terms in the college, he was dismissed suddenly by the president for what was termed "refusal to obey orders." He was charged with not closing the chapel windows, as the president had sent a bearer to instruct him to do. The fact was that the bearer never delivered the message, but no excuse was accepted and Leo-Rhynie was sent home. The following year he wanted to begin all over again but was told he must wait six months more. Let him tell the rest of the story:

"I was enveloped in a cloud of sorrow and doubt, but I obeyed. There was always an overmastering urge and assurance that God had called me, and even these disappointments were his appointments. I reappeared at the college the following September and was admitted. Every stumbling block became a stepping-stone. At my ordination on October 24, 1932, the president of the college said, 'I am happy to say that it was the pleasure of the college staff to watch and admire the student life of Mr. Leo-Rhynie and to share his fellowship at college. We are confident he will be a good minister of our Lord Jesus Christ.' God opens doors before prepared people, and those who honor him, he honors. To him be the glory."

Two years after his ordination, Leo-Rhynie married Winifred Chin, and they are the parents of four children, all of whom are active in Christian work. Mrs. Leo-Rhynie serves on the Executive Committee of the North American Baptist Woman's Union, and she and her husband were in London in 1955, and later in Rio de Janeiro and Miami Beach for congresses of the Baptist World Alliance. They have traveled in the United States and many other lands in the interest of missions and the work of the Jamaica Baptist Missionary Society.

Meanwhile, the work at East Queen Street has prospered, as did his two previous pastorates. Since 1958, the membership has doubled and maintains a fully graded Sunday School.

He is held in high esteem by all his fellow ministers who say of him:

"His has been a happy blend of Christian dignity and humility . . . and we are proud that we have a Christian leader second to none in caliber in Jamaica's church life. He is a man who inspires confidence." He himself says, "Ever since the day of my birth, I have been receiving so much that I am weighed down with the burden of my indebtedness to everyone far and near; and yet I have so little to give. Nevertheless, I have given my all to him who gave up all for me."

In addition to his pastorate and other responsibilities in the community, Leo-Rhynie also serves as chaplain of the general penitentiary in Jamaica. His ministry there is appreciated by authorities and inmates alike. Under his leadership his church has just built the first Christian educational center in Jamaica, demonstrating anew that faith in God makes possible that which seems utterly impossible and that no man attains his best without great enthusiasm. One of his favorite verses says, "It shall be done."

THE ORIENT

THE ORIENT

Burma

William and Marian Hackett

What a debt we owe to those who translate the
Word of God into a language we can understand. I came to
appreciate this anew when I met Mrs. William Hackett in
Burma. She and her husband were missionaries of the American Baptist Convention until all missionaries were ordered
by the government to leave the country.

Marian Hackett is a lovely person and a charming hostess.
Handicapped by frequent illnesses, with great dedication she
has given her life to translating the Scriptures so that the
people of Burma can have the Word of God in their own
tongue. Adoniram Judson did this work long ago, but, as in
our own land, so in Burma, there must be continuing transla-
tions and revisions. In addition, the gospel must be translated
into a wide variety of local dialects.

Mrs. Hackett explained how she and national pastors and
scholars would gather to talk over the translation of a passage
of Scripture. After consultation about the meaning of the passage, they would work independently and again come together
to discuss each word and phrase. Then they would seek to
reconcile differences in order to arrive at the best possible text.
Their final translation would then be submitted to another

group of scholars to be sure that it was as accurate as possible. This is a slow and painstaking work, but it is being done in many lands by mission and Bible societies.

While Mrs. Hackett gives herself to translating the Word into a living language, her husband carries on the work of evangelism, taking the Word to others and living it day by day. How effective his work has been can be illustrated by the witness of one Baptist congregation to which he ministered.

Shortly after the end of the Japanese invasion of Burma, Bill Hackett went in his jeep seeking a lost congregation—that is, they were lost to him but not to the Lord! They had moved often to avoid capture by the Japanese and had faced many trials and difficulties. Finally, he found them back in the hills and was appalled at their condition. Their clothes were torn and worn and tattered. Many were sick and all were gaunt from hunger.

Overwhelmed by it all, he said, "I shall be back again next week. Tell me what you most need and I'll load my jeep and bring it to you." In Baptist fashion, they had a congregational meeting to talk it over and decide. Finally, they told him, "We have learned to live without too much food. Our clothes will last a little longer. We need Bibles and hymnbooks. We lost most of ours in travels and frequent hasty moves, and we need them so that we can teach our children the Word of God and worship together." Bill Hackett and his wife and others had taught them so well that, above all else, they cherished the Bread of life to feed their souls.

A few years later Mrs. Hackett became seriously ill again and the doctors advised earnestly that she return to the United States for diagnosis and treatment. She did not want to leave her husband, but if she did leave in the face of uncertain conditions, she wanted to be sure she could get back into Burma. The Hacketts made it a matter of prayer; and, to their great joy, she was granted the first reentry visa that had been issued for months. However, she must return within a specified time.

Would she be well enough to return within the time limit? This, too, was made a matter of prayer. After some months at home, she wrote with great joy, "I'm well enough to go back within the time and I'll be with Bill for Christmas."

Once again, faith was justified. The Hacketts were together again and the work went on. He was busy with the churches and she was hard at work again translating, with her co-laborers, the Word of life.

Now that all Baptist missionaries have been compelled to leave Burma, the Hacketts have the joy of knowing that they have left behind them many faithful believers and countless copies of the Bible with the truth that makes men free.

Hong Kong

Lam Chi Fung

Hong Kong is one of the most remarkable cities in the world, situated as it is on the border of Red China and built around a marvelous port that attracts the commerce of the world. In Hong Kong lives a remarkable man, Lam Chi Fung. "Dr. Lam," as he is called by all who know and love him, is really "Mr. Baptist" in Hong Kong. He is a man of deep faith and great consecration.

When I asked Dr. Lam to share his secret with others, this is what he said:

"God has always been very kind to me and, throughout all the years, he has bestowed on me many blessings. So I have come to love him all the more. There are two blessings I would like to mention especially. The first was over forty years ago when I was afflicted with a terrible sickness which kept me in bed for two months. I prayed to the Lord with all my heart for his watchcare over me, and I fully recovered my health and strength. The second blessing came when World War II ended and peace was restored. I returned to Hong Kong as a man who had lost all his material possessions. However, by the grace of God, difficult circumstances gradually improved and I met with success after success in all that I undertook to do.

100

These two incidents show you what God has meant to me."

Business success has certainly been his. He is managing director of the Sze Wai Company, the Hong Kong Chiap Hua Manufacturing Company, the Ka Wah Bank, and the Chik Fung Investments Company. These and other business interests he has now turned over to his sons, and he gives his full time to Christian work.

In the religious field this remarkable man serves as chairman of the United Hong Kong Baptist Association and the treasurer of the Hong Kong Chinese Christian Churches Union. He is chairman of the deacons of the Kowloon Baptist Church, which has just completed construction of its own new air-conditioned building. Formerly, he served as president of the Chinese Young Men's Christian Association and was a member of the Board of Education in Hong Kong.

In the heart of Kowloon stands Pui Ching Middle School, a great high school with some twenty-five hundred students. Dr. Lam serves as its principal. Sensing the need of a college for Baptist young people, he organized and became the president of the Hong Kong Baptist College, a growing institution with tremendous possibilities. He also has been a leader in raising the funds and building a fine new Baptist hospital in Hong Kong to meet the growing needs of this city's vast hordes of refugees and its teeming population.

In recognition of his outstanding public service, Dr. Lam has been awarded the Order of Dragon by the Annamese Government. He has also been honored with the British Coronation Medal and the Order of the British Empire. In 1955, he received an honorary degree of Doctor of Laws from Oklahoma Baptist University in the United States and in 1965 received an honorary degree from Stetson University in Florida.

Dr. Lam attended the Ninth Baptist World Congress in London where he was elected a vice-president. He also was present at the Tenth Congress in Rio de Janeiro and the Eleventh Congress in Miami Beach. On these tours he has visited many parts of the world, but he was especially interested in visiting the Middle East. There he fulfilled the desire of many years, to see for himself the places he had read about in the Scriptures and to visit some of the places where the Christian faith began.

What is the secret of such a life? Dr. Lam was born in a Christian home in 1892, in Kityang, Kwangtung Province, China. His father was minister of the Baptist church, and he was trained in Christian schools. A Christian home and Christian education led him to make his own profession of Christ as Saviour and to become a devoted follower of Christ as Lord.

Dr. and Mrs. Lam have been blessed with six sons and two daughters, most of whom have received higher education in America. To be in their home and to sense the love and loyalty of his family is a blessing to anyone. In spite of the heavy pressure of work, Dr. Lam has regular periods every day for Bible study and prayer. This is where he gets the strength and energy to carry on his outstanding work for Christ in the city where he has been so blessed materially.

When we visited Hong Kong in 1956, Dr. Lam was again in the hospital, critically ill. When we entered the hospital room, his face lighted with a smile and he welcomed us gladly. After we had voiced our concern about his illness, he asked us to pray for him. We bowed our heads and lifted our hearts in prayer, asking God to raise his servant up to continue the good work to which he was so fully committed. Our prayers and those of others were answered and he was soon well and strong again.

Hong Kong

Rosalind Lam

       Henrietta Hall Shuck is a familiar name to many Baptists in this land and others. She is known as the first Baptist woman to serve as a missionary in China, where she gave her life after a few short years of dedicated service as a Christian homemaker and teacher.

The work of Christian education that she began in her own home is continued today in the Henrietta School in Hong Kong, not far from Happy Valley Cemetery where Henrietta Shuck was buried. Her name and her spirit live on in a beautiful modern school for girls, headed by Rosalind Lam.

How did such a school and such a building come about? The answer is largely in the vision and dedication of one Christian woman, although, of course, there have been many others who have shared in the realization of her dream. Let Rosalind Lam tell you her own story in her own words, bearing in mind that she represents many other Christian women who are giving themselves to the cause of Christian education as well as the building of Christian homes.

"I thank God for giving me an opportunity to tell about the unceasing love and grace which He has bestowed upon me. I was born into a family of eight. My father, Mr. Wong Kwok-

Shuen, is the oldest deacon still serving in the Hong Kong Baptist Church. My late mother, Mrs. Wong Tong Cheong-Ling, was the daughter of the Rev. Tong Kit-Hing. She was one of the first two women ordained deaconesses in 1930, and she was one of the pioneers in Christian education in Hong Kong.

"My parents' faithfulness to God and love for Him and man gave an unforgettable example of a true Christian. Every Sunday, we were taken to Sunday School, unless we were sick; and we enjoyed the Bible stories and hymns very much. Once my brother and I were asked to sing at a Christmas celebration. Although we had stage fright, we were joyful after the song ended, because we knew that we had passed the message of Christ's birth to the congregation. From my own experience, I have come to realize the importance of bringing children to Sunday School, for what they learn from the Bible and the singing of hymns will always be imprinted in their minds.

"When I came to choosing a life partner, God answered my prayers by giving me an understanding husband, Mr. Lam Chik-Suen, who has helped me through many disappointments and difficulties. God has also blessed us with three children, the eldest of whom is now working. My sister-in-law, Mrs. Edna Wong, and many other friends have been a source of encouragement and help to me through their prayers and advice. For all these, I give thanks to my Heavenly Father.

"Since 1952, God has given me the opportunity to serve Him in the field of Christian education in the Henrietta School. It is a coeducational school, founded in memory of a loving, gallant, and devoted Christian, Mrs. Henrietta Hall Shuck, who was the wife of the Rev. Lewis Shuck. In this school, I have learned many invaluable lessons of how to work with others, and, most important of all, that nothing is impossible in the hands of God.

"For the construction of our present school building, we had to pay the contractor by instalments. When the seventh instalment was almost due, I discovered that the amount left in our account was only one tenth of what we had to pay. I tried in vain every possible means to obtain money, and as the day drew closer and closer, I became so worried that night after night I cried myself to sleep.

"One night, while I was thus worrying and crying, I seemed to hear a still small voice, rebuking my foolishness for not committing my burden to God. Although it was cold and in the middle of the night, I got up and knelt beside my bed. . . . After my prayer, . . . I fell asleep.

"A few days later, I was informed by James Belote of the Southern Baptist Mission Board that donations had been sent to our school from the First Baptist Church of Richmond, Virginia, and by Mrs. Thomas Stanley of Virginia in memory of her mother, Mrs. Bassett. The pleasant surprise could not but fill my heart with unsurpassable joy and deep gratitude to my Heavenly Father for answering my prayers.

"Indeed, God knows everything. He knows our needs, and all we have to do is to go to him with our troubles and difficulties and he will surely help us according to his ways and time."

Such is the witness of this Christian mother and educator. Truly, she has learned that the words of the psalmist are true: "Goodness and mercy shall follow me all the days of my life." Hundreds of girls have already felt the touch of her spirit and the impress of her faith. The work begun by Henrietta Hall Shuck, in her own home years ago, still goes on through the dedication of Rosalind Lam, who is willing to take time from her home that others may have Christian homes of their own.

India

Alice R. Veeraswamy

Our hospitality was really put to the test when
Alice Veeraswamy came to visit in our home. As a teacher in
a Christian school in India, she was interested in studying
Christian education in this country and in visiting American
homes and churches. When Mrs. Adams was helping Alice get
settled in her room, she said, "Now, we want you to feel right
at home. If there is anything we can do for you, or that you
would like to do, please let us know."

Many hostesses have said that to guests many times. Alice
smiled and asked, "Do you really mean that?" Taken aback,
Mrs. Adams said, "Why, of course I do. What would you like
to do?"

Our Indian guest replied, "I have often wondered in visiting
in other homes in this country what you American women keep
in all these closed closets and drawers and cupboards that I
see. Even in your land of abundance, I cannot imagine what
you have that could fill so many storage places."

That, I submit, is a real test of hospitality! But, without any
hesitation, Mrs. Adams said, "Why, of course, you may open
any closet, any cupboard, any drawer and see for yourself."
And Miss Veeraswamy did just that. She literally went over

the whole house. She opened up every drawer and door. She could hardly believe what she saw. Finally, in amazement she said, "You American women have so much and the women in my country have so little. Surely God has blessed you abundantly. Surely he expects much of you as you serve others."

Hers was a memorable and unforgettable visit, and our friendship has continued through the years. We met her only once more. That was in Royal Albert Hall in London, during the Baptist World Congress in 1955. We have kept in touch every year, through letters at Christmas and at other times, for we have been keenly interested in what this Christian teacher and her associates are doing in a land that is striving to make the most of its independence.

This dedicated Christian teacher has gone on, teaching one school generation after another, helping to train Christian women in her homeland for a new and better tomorrow. She is very proud of her former students and has kept in personal touch with scores of them. Many who have sensed her dedication and have been touched by her warm heart and radiant spirit now fill places of leadership in church and community.

A few years ago, a critical illness confined her to the hospital for many weeks. When her brother finally was told he could take her home, the doctor warned, "She may not even survive the journey home, and if she does, she undoubtedly will die before the end of the year."

In a few months, Miss Veeraswamy was back at her place of teaching. So great is her faith and courage! She had to wear a support for her back as she traveled through the rough streets of the city, but in her last year of teaching she was the only one on the staff who never missed a day because of illness, although she was the oldest teacher in the group.

To help her friends understand her dedication to Christian education, she wrote in her Christmas letter some years ago:

Never before has the significance of a Christian school been brought home to me, as it has been in these days, when I realize the schoolchildren of today are the nation-builders of tomorrow. As such, the very best of ideals should be set before them.

Last month a former student of our school, a Hindu girl now a mother of two children, lay dying of tuberculosis. On her bed of pain, she wanted to hear again the stories of Jesus she once heard at school over ten years before. I thought it was similar to the heart's cry of Simon Peter: "Lord, to whom shall we go? Thou hast the words of eternal life." Incidents such as these keep my faith in a Christian school alive, strong, and growing.

Alice was born in a Christian home and grew from childhood in the knowledge of Jesus Christ. She writes:

During my early years and youth, I closely watched with wonder the selfless and loving service of Miss Frances Tencate and Dr. Lena Benjamin and there grew within me a desire to serve my own people with the same fervor and devotion as the two women I came to know. Service in a Christian school afforded me an opportunity to have my desire fufilled.

The prayer life of my mother all the time we have lived together has impressed me very much. To her, God is a real person. Her simple childlike faith in God is evident every day in our home.

After my acceptance of Christ as my Saviour, at the time of my baptism, when I was ten years of age, I dedicated my life to him. There have been several times in my life since when I have rededicated my life to his service.

Surely, we can thank God for women like Alice Veeraswamy who dedicate all they are and all that they have in quiet, faithful, and humble service for the Master—and who count it their greatest joy to teach others the lessons they have learned from the Master Teacher of us all.

Indonesia

Ais Pormes

Southern Baptist mission work in Indonesia began in 1951, when W. B. Johnson and two other missionaries arrived in Djákarta. All three had formerly been missionaries in China, but since it was impossible to continue work on the mainland, they had gone, at the request of the Foreign Mission Board, to see about starting Baptist work in this new area. They were confident that they could gather a group of believers in a fairly short time, but they were deeply concerned about how they could find and train national leaders for the churches.

Eager to begin, they rented a building and put up a sign, indicating that it was a Southern Baptist mission. One day, to their amazement and delight, an Indonesian appeared on the scene and told them he was a Baptist pastor with a congregation that met in his home. How did he happen to be there, and what was the story behind Ais Pormes, the pastor who, in the providence of God, was on the field and ready to serve?

Here is his story, as I have learned it from Mrs. W. B. Johnson, for many years a missionary in Indonesia with her husband until their retirement.

"January 19, 1944, was a hot day on this little Island of Serua in the Banda Sea, for it is only about five degrees from the equator. The Japanese occupied all the large islands around. On this memorable day, seven American planes came to bomb Ambon, the capital of the Mollucas. One plane had trouble and crashed into the sea near Serua and the men were floating around in the sea on life rafts.

"Fortunately for these men, most of the people on this island were Christians and had been taught that Christians should love all men everywhere. In the group who watched the plane crash was a young man, whose name was Ais [ice] Pormes, nicknamed "Preacher" by all his playmates, because he once answered a question in Sunday School when none of the rest could.

"It was Ais who said to the watching crowd, 'Let's get some canoes and go out and save those men.' With valiant efforts they were able to save five men and row them to safety. 'There were fear and anguish as well as suffering on the faces of these men. When we got them ashore, I asked the pilot if he knew Jesus.' The word for Jesus in Indonesian is so similar to the English that the pilot understood it and nodded his head that he did. Then the pilot turned and asked me, 'Do you know Jesus?' I smiled and nodded my head that I did. Then there was an expression of great relief and peace on his face. [At this time Ais knew no English and these men knew no Indonesian.]

"All the men had swollen limbs and two of them had to be carried on stretchers. We used an old remedy that our people have used for many years. You pound or grate a coconut, pour boiling water on it, then squeeze out all the substance you can. To this coconut milk add salt and use it to make hot compresses to take out the swelling. At first the men screamed with pain, but we assured them it would be better tomorrow.

"The two men on stretchers were very sick, so I sent some of the women to our home to get mattresses and sheets to fix beds for them and make them as comfortable as possible. The old ladies cooked rice, fish, and other food for them. The young men gathered bananas, papayas, and many other kinds of fruit.

"A group of us slept out on the beach with the rescued fliers that night. After midnight, I woke up, chilly from the sea breeze coming in. I got up and hunted for sticks and leaves to make a fire. Others joined me and we soon had a nice, big bonfire going. We sat around the bonfire and began to sing hymns. Since it wasn't long after Christmas, I started singing 'Silent Night.' As we sang in Indonesian, the Americans joined us, singing in English. After that we sang 'What a Friend We Have in Jesus' and many other hymns.

"After the bonfire and Christian fellowship in singing, we slept some more. At 5:30 the next morning, just at dawn, we were suddenly awakened by the roar of a plane overhead. We realized that this plane had come to find and pick up the American aviators. Three other fellows and I indicated we would like to go too. So we helped take the two sick men on the amphibious plane. Still wearing our pajamas, we flew off on the wings of the morning into the blue sky, and after about seven or eight hours set down in Darwin, Australia.

"The Americans were taken to an American hospital. They took us to the camp for Indonesians. From there we were sent to Melbourne to have an interview with the Dutch Intelligence officers. I was invited to join the Australian Intelligence Corps.

"In one month I picked up a lot of English. I used the Bible as a textbook and learned words and phrases by comparing the English and Indonesian.

"Somehow my playmates calling me 'Preacher' had made me

think a lot about being one. I really wanted to be a preacher, but since my father died when I was fourteen years old and I was the oldest son, I had to support my mother and the rest of the family. There were five sisters, two brothers, and two grandparents besides my mother. Three sisters were older, but in those days there was no way for girls to earn money. So much of the time I worked all day and studied at night.

"Once I had a good job as bookkeeper of the Singer Sewing Machine Company in Ambon. One night while I was counting the money, I seemed to hear a quiet voice say, 'You are counting millions of rupiahs while millions of souls are dying without knowing me.' That night a stanza of a hymn kept ringing in my mind and heart:

> E'er since by faith I saw the stream
> Thy flowing wounds supply,
> Redeeming love has been my theme,
> And shall be till I die.

"Then I said, 'Lord, if you want me to be a witness like that, please open the way for me.'

"When the war was over I was alerted to return to Djakarta within a week. Meanwhile, I had a telegram from Melbourne. My boss in the Intelligence Corps was editor of an Indonesian newspaper there and wanted me to help him. I worked in the morning and studied English at home in the afternoons.

"During this time, on my way to and from the office, I passed the headquarters of a Christian organization called Campaigners for Christ. I was hungry for Christian fellowship and wanted very much to join them but was very timid about entering alone. One day I got up my courage and went in. They gave me a very warm welcome. I went with them on many open-air preaching trips.

"One night, we held a meeting with the servicemen. I was asked to say a few words. My few feeble words seemed to touch their hearts. Afterwards, the secretary asked me to visit him, which I did. He invited me to go with him to the Keswick Convention. There I met many Christians. I suddenly found myself changed from a lonely soldier to a loved and much-sought-after Christian. In the Keswick Convention, I met many Christian leaders. From these friends, I got my inspiration to go to the Melbourne Bible Institute. When I inquired about studying there, Superintendent Robinson said, 'We like you but don't believe you can make it with your limited English. However, we will think about it.'

"I was transferred from the Newspaper to the Film Department. When I got my dismissal from there, the officer gave me a good letter of recommendation. I went from there to the Campaigners for Christ headquarters. As I entered the lobby, the telephone was ringing. The president of the Bible school was calling for me. He said, 'We have been praying for you. Are you coming?' 'I'll be there today in time for tea,' I told him.

"Before I finished at the Bible Institute, I found a catalog from Moody Bible School in Chicago. I was so interested in it, I wrote about studying there. They advised me I would have to have three or four thousand dollars. This I did not have.

"Dr. Hyman Appleman, a converted American Jew, came to Australia to hold some evangelistic meetings. I went to see him and told him I wanted to study in a seminary in the U. S. A. He wrote to the Bible Institute in Los Angeles for me. They sent me a catalog and application blank and said they would guarantee me work while I was there. As soon as the Lord revealed that plan to me, I booked passage to San Francisco—actually nine months before I sailed.

"My visa and papers didn't come through until two hours before my train left for Sydney. The Immigration Department had required a deposit of eighty pounds when I had enrolled as a student. When I requested it to be returned, they said they would mail it to the boat company. It didn't get there until the day to leave Melbourne. I was ready to leave when a man called and said it had come. When I went for it, they said it couldn't be changed into U. S. money, as there was a shortage at that time. I asked to see the manager of the bank. I went into his office and was surprised to find a man who had fought in the war in Indonesia. He had been in Ambon and named the street my family once lived on. We talked a few minutes and then he fixed up the money for me. Again the Lord had gone before and prepared the way for me. I caught the last train that would get me to Sydney before the boat sailed.

"After I arrived in San Francisco, I was waiting in the Customhouse for my baggage when two gentlemen came up. A friend in Australia had written them to meet me. They got me a place to stay until I went on to Los Angeles.

"By studying winter and summer, I finished the four-year course at the Bible Institute in Los Angeles in three years. It was during this time that I became a Baptist. The government allowed me to stay another year to get practical Christian training or to travel and speak. The Lord has marvelously led me every step of the way.

"The crashing of that plane and the riding out on the wings of the morning was just as Isaiah 42:16 says: 'I will lead them in paths that they have not known: I will make darkness light before them, and crooked things straight. These things will I do unto them, and not forsake them.' Through all these experiences God had heard and answered my prayers."

When Ais Pormes returned to Indonesia, he organized a small congregation that met in his own home. Soon after, he was walking down the street and saw the sign of the Southern Baptist mission. Going in, he introduced himself as a Baptist and invited the missionaries to come and worship with him and his congregation the next Sunday night. Since they had a building and no congregation, they were happy, indeed, to do it—and to their joy they found a fine Baptist group of forty. They invited the group to worship with them the next Sunday night, though they were hardly prepared for so many. The next Sunday, in spite of rain, twenty-seven came. In November, 1953, the building was completed and the new congregation was all ready to move in.

When the time came to open the hospital work in Indonesia, there was difficulty, but the government finally gave permission. Mr. Pormes went with Mr. Johnson to Kediri and they finally located an ideal spot in a coconut grove. However, the owner refused to sell.

After a long conversation, Mr. Pormes finally said to Mr. Johnson, "You and Dr. Jones go back to the hotel and rest tonight. Let me talk to this man by myself, and maybe I can persuade him." The next morning he said very simply, "Well, he agreed to sell it to you for the hospital."

Thus began Baptist medical work in Indonesia. Mr. Pormes went on to keep his promise to serve with another Christian group, but, in the providence of God, he was ready at just the right time to help Baptists begin one of their most promising mission fields, in a land where both Moslems and Christians are carrying on extensive mission work and millions of lives are at stake.

Japan

Shuichi Matsumura

Shuichi Matsumura, pastor of the Tokiwadai Baptist Church in Tokyo, has been under Christian influence all his life. It is no surprise then that he was asked to be director of the New Life Movement in Japan which brought genuine new life and hope and the thrilling realization of possible victory to the Baptists of Japan.

Shuichi's parents were baptized by one of the first Southern Baptist missionaries in Japan, and his mother took Shuichi to all the meetings of the church that she attended. Later he studied at Seinan Gakuin, and graduated from Seinan Seminary in 1938.

A three-year period of service in the Japanese Army was a time of confused thought for the young Christian. When he finally left the army, he decided to go into secular work and was employed by the Mitsui Coal Mine Company. He was very active in organizing labor unions during this early period of his life.

During this time he married Nobuko Kawakatsu, a daughter of the very first Japanese to be ordained a Baptist minister by Southern Baptists. As a good Christian wife, Nobuko helped her husband find a renewed faith in Christ and a new dedica-

116

tion to Christian service. Before long they started holding weekly Christian services in their home. In three years' time the cottage meeting grew to be a big mission point, and Shuichi's ministry began to attract attention.

In 1949, the senior pastors of the Japan Baptist Convention recognized his ability as an organizer and asked him to serve as the general secretary of the Convention. This meant moving to Tokyo, where he served as general secretary from 1949 to 1951. At heart, however, he was still a pastor, and while giving full time to his responsibilities as secretary, he continued to hold services in his own home. Finally, with the assistance of funds from the Lottie Moon Christmas offering, the little congregation was able to build its own building and in three years the Tokiwadai Baptist Church became one of the ten largest churches in Tokyo.

The call of the pastorate was so strong that in 1952 Matsumura decided to give his full time to the ministry of the Tokiwadai Church. In that same year, his beloved and dedicated Christian wife died, leaving Shuichi with three small children. So, in addition to the responsibilities of the church, he had the full care of the three little ones.

In the providence of God he agreed the next year, even with these heavy responsibilities, to serve as chairman of the Youth Committee of the Japan Baptist Convention. Here he came to know Akiko Endo who was serving as the youth secretary for the Convention. God had been preparing Akiko for definite Christian service, and Shuichi decided the Lord had also prepared her to be his wife—and in a short time they were married.

Akiko, unlike her husband, was not raised in a Christian home. Her conversion actually infuriated her father so much that he said she must either give up the Christian faith or leave home. Choosing to follow Christ, Akiko left home and went to the missionary friend who had won her to Christ as Saviour and Lord. This good missionary, Dorothy Carver, a daughter of W. O. Carver of the Southern Baptist Seminary in Louisville, took Akiko to her heart and said, "You are my child."

Akiko had always been independent. She loved to study, but her desire to go to college was completely ignored by the family who believed that higher education was only for boys. She had been taught from birth that the youngest daughter of the family is expected to be obedient—to parents and to big sister and brothers. When Akiko insisted on added education, her parents finally sent her to a short-term English conversation school on the second floor of the Tokyo YMCA. It was there that she first met Dorothy Carver, who taught in a language school on the same floor. Casual conversation developed into regular Bible study, and after a year of careful study and thought, Akiko accepted Christ as Saviour and Lord.

Now she must make her own way in the world, and she and Miss Carver decided that she should attend Kwassui Woman's College, a Christian school in Nagasaki. Akiko was especially gifted in languages and wanted to use her talents to serve her Lord. She graduated just as World War II began and stayed on at the college as a teacher of English. Just a few months before the second atomic bomb was dropped on Nagasaki, she fortunately was called home and was reconciled to her parents after six years of separation.

Two years after the war ended, Akiko went as one of the first four students granted permission to leave the occupied country of Japan. She was to attend the Training School established by Woman's Missionary Union in Louisville. There she came under the personal guidance of W. O. Carver, who one day said to her, "I know you can do it. God has made an investment in you."

In 1950 she returned to Japan to become youth secretary of her Convention and later to serve as editor of Training Union quarterlies and on the editorial staff of the New Life Movement and the Jordan Press, publishing house of the Japan Baptist Convention. From 1950 to 1960, she also served on the Youth Committee of the Baptist World Alliance.

The decision to marry Shuichi Matsumura was a difficult one. She would be marrying her boss, for he was chairman of the Youth Committee for which she worked. She had no confidence that she could become a good mother to his three children. However, love prevailed and Shuichi and Akiko have served wonderfully together through the years since their marriage in May, 1954.

As leader of the New Life Movement, Shuichi Matsumura made a significant contribution to Baptist life in his own land and also was welcomed and honored by Baptists in the United States, where he visited in the interest of aiding efforts to win his homeland to Christ.

At the Baptist World Congress at Miami Beach, Florida, in June of 1965, Shuichi was elected a vice-president of the Baptist World Alliance—a fitting recognition of his growth in Christian faith and service. Akiko was elected the same year to serve as vice-president of the Woman's Missionary Union of the Japan Baptist Convention. All three of the children have become Christians, and their bond of love and affection has proved enduring through all the pressures of life. Surely Shuichi and Akiko illustrate beautifully what two people can mean to each other and to the work of the kingdom of God when they love the Lord with all their hearts and seek to do his will.

The Philippines

President Magsaysay

"President Magsaysay will see us today if we can be there in fifteen minutes," said Missionary Ted Badger excitedly as he rushed into the Baptist Book Store in Manila.

When we drove into the palace grounds, it was evident that the people had taken their president at his word. Individuals and family groups wandered over the grounds, enjoying their beauty. Inside the palace we found a host of people, many poorly dressed and with bare feet. In the halls and on the staircases and in every room we saw people—some working, others talking or waiting.

We were ushered into a private parlor, beautifully furnished, where we were asked to wait for a little while. Another group—wives of members of the Rotary Club of Manila—was also waiting to see the president. They wanted his support for a charity project in which they were interested. We got to talk with some of them and explain who we were and why we were there. We took advantage of every opportunity to say a word about our Baptist people.

Soon an usher told us the president would see us. Expecting to be ushered into a quiet, private office, we were surprised when the door opened and we stepped into an adjacent room crowded with people. They were standing around in various groups and delegations.

The president greeted us warmly, and after the usual handshakes and picture-taking, we talked briefly about our Baptist work in the Philippines and he assured us of his concern for full religious freedom for all believers. He himself was a devout Roman Catholic but believed in freedom of conscience and full freedom for religion in the new independent country he was helping to create.

As we left, there was a moment I shall never forget. As I shook his hand to say good-bye, I said, "Mr. President, I shall be praying for you in the days ahead as you face your big responsibility here in the Philippines."

His whole mood changed at once. A smile left his face. Deeply touched, he gripped my hand anew and said, "Sir, do pray for me. How I need it." There we stood for a brief unforgettable moment—Catholic and Baptist together—each of us had bared his heart to the other. I saw a man whose shoulders drooped with the heavy responsibilities he bore and who realized then as never before how much he needed the help of Almighty God.

As I left his office, we waved to each other. The smile was back on his face as he turned to meet another group. But I knew I had met a man—a man seeking to serve God and his fellowmen. None of us knew then that all too soon his life was to be ended tragically. In just a few weeks he was killed in a plane crash as he flew in the southern part of the Philippines to visit some of his people.

I shall not soon forget the depth of conviction and feeling of the one who put into words the need of us all, "Do pray for me. How I need it."

The World

Our Baptist World Fellowship

Singing of the stirring hymn "All Hail the Power of Jesus' Name" opens each Baptist World Congress. Those who attend never forget the inspiration of that hour. Thousands, each in his own tongue, join in exalting the same Lord and sense anew a oneness in Jesus Christ.

Our Baptist World Fellowship is far more real and vital than an organization, though we do have that. It is people—twenty-seven million of them—from one hundred countries, representing every continent on the globe. Yet, each is an individual for whom Christ died and each is a professed and baptized believer in Jesus Christ as Saviour and Lord.

As we look briefly at our theme, the second word calls to mind great champions of the faith: John the Baptist; John Bunyan; John Clifford; the beloved John MacNeill, who, in 1929, said, "Never was our witness as Baptists more needed than today. Never was our task more clearly defined. We are a New Testament people. The authority of God's Holy Word, the deity of Christ, the sufficiency of his atoning sacrifice, the need and hope of regeneration, the miracle of his resurrection, the potency of his living presence, the competency of the soul to deal directly with God through Christ, the enshrining of these great truths in the baptism he has left us, the assertion of Christ's claims in every relationship of men and nations . . . these are the cardinal notes of our witness."

Many other names, of course, are called to mind by the word "Baptist." We think of William Carey and his pioneer missionary work in India; Adoniram Judson and the beginning of a wonderful Baptist work in Burma; Roger Williams, who pioneered for the Baptists in North America; J. M. Rushbrooke, Walter Lewis, Arnold Ohrn, and Josef Nordenhaug, beloved secretaries of the Alliance through the years. Each of these men made a distinctive contribution to Baptist life and work.

"Jesus Christ, the same yesterday, today, and forever." In 1908, John Clifford put it this way: "We have said, and we still need to say, that each church is independent of every other church, and independent of any caste of priests or ministers . . . a perfect and complete organization and, with Christ as its ruler, fully competent to manage itself. But we organize for worldwide cooperation and complete abandonment to the spirit and purpose of the catholicity of the gospel of Christ, encouraged in our adherence to these principles by seeing that the gravitation of the thought and conviction of the churches of Christ is distinctly, and with growing strength, toward those ideas of Christ and his gospel for which we stand."

This is beautifully illustrated at the Roll Call of the Nations, which is an important part of every Baptist World Congress. At the Tenth Congress in Rio de Janeiro, in 1960, a representative of each nation where Baptists are serving came, with the flag of his country, to the platform to be greeted by the Alliance president. Then, in his own tongue, he repeated the Congress theme, "That at the name of Jesus every knee should bow and every tongue confess that Jesus Christ is Lord, to the glory of

God the Father." It was a moving and unforgettable experience
for all who had the privilege of sharing in it. With more feeling,
perhaps, than ever before we could sing—

> All hail the power of Jesus' name!
> Let angels prostrate fall;
> Bring forth the royal diadem,
> And crown Him Lord of all.

Ours is a *world* fellowship of Baptists. We are to be found
literally around the world, on every continent and in most countries. We serve the Lord Christ under varying conditions. Some
are under totalitarian governments and others in democracies.
Some serve where there are state churches and others where
free churches predominate. Some are suffering hardship for
Christ, while others have full freedom to preach and teach the
faith we cherish.

Let me give you a brief glimpse of some of these Baptists in
various lands.

There are over half a million baptized believers in Baptist
churches in Russia. Under severe hardship and many difficulties, they continue their work of evangelism, proclaiming what
they rightly call "New Testament Christianity." They bear their
witness all over the Soviet Union in over five thousand
churches.

In Burma all Baptist missionaries have been ordered to leave,
but the two hundred thousand Burmese Baptists will continue
to witness for Christ, regardless of government policies. One
of the most remarkable churches I know is the Immanuel Baptist Church in Rangoon, where every Sunday services are held
at different hours in five different languages. It was a thrilling
experience for me to worship in that church and to conduct the
Lord's Supper at the English service late one Sunday afternoon.

In the Philippines it was my privilege to speak at the Central Baptist College at Iloilo, where students from all over the islands prepare themselves for places as Christian leaders. Each spring, a series of evangelistic services is concluded with a baptismal service in an outdoor baptistry in front of the Administration Building on the campus. This traditional service is continued as a public witness to those who may never darken a church door.

The Baptist World Alliance is a voluntary and fraternal organization for promoting fellowship and cooperation among Baptists. It is neither an administrative body for sending missionaries, nor a legislative body, nor a judicial body. It has no authority over any convention or local church. It seeks to express and promote unity and fellowship among Baptists of the world, to provide assistance and relief when needed, to secure and defend religious freedom, and to proclaim the great principles of our common faith.

It meets ordinarily every five years in a World Congress, though world conditions or war sometimes causes postponement. The executive committee, the officers and staff, departments, and commissions carry on the work year by year.

The Alliance operates through a fine and growing Women's Department in which many able Baptist women find opportunities for fellowship and service. The Youth Department holds a World Youth Conference every five years, the last two in Toronto, Canada, and Beirut, Lebanon. There is also a growing Men's Department that will challenge our men to follow the man Christ Jesus.

During crises, the Relief Department of the Alliance feeds and clothes the hungry, cares for refugees, and helps them find new places of security and opportunity. Who could forget the marvelous outpouring of Christian love and concern at the Copenhagen Congress, when for the first time many met refugees face to face. Gladly each gave all he could spare, and more, of his clothing and other necessities of life.

For a number of years, between world congresses, the Alliance has carried on a program of study commissions. Representative theologians and other leaders from many conventions provide a cross-fertilization of ideas, a deepening of convictions, and a means of strengthening our work in many areas.

The commissions are: Religious Liberty and Human Relations, Evangelism and Missions, Doctrine of the Church, and Bible Study and Membership Training. Each commission makes a report at the Congress and also prepares study documents.

The Baptist World, published each month by the Baptist World Alliance, carries information about Baptists in many lands. The Baptist World Press is an information service to supply other news media items of interest to Baptists everywhere.

This is *our* Baptist World Fellowship. It is ours—ours to appreciate and profit from, ours to share with others, ours to pass on to coming generations—the stronger and the better because of our contribution to it. It is ours because we are Christ's and we are one in him and in the fellowship of all who love and serve him.

What is it that holds us together when we have so many differences and diversities?

It is our shared convictions—convictions that command our loyalty and call us to service. We share a common conviction in the lordship of Christ. The early Christians identified themselves to other believers with the simple statement, "Jesus Christ is Lord." Through the years, that sense of fellowship in him has been a source of strength and assurance.

In Czechoslovakia some years ago, I worshiped in one of our little churches and shared in the Lord's Supper. There, in a land dominated by Communist thought, we shared the symbols of the body and blood of our Lord and sang together "Blessed Assurance, Jesus Is Mine."

We share a conviction that the Bible is God's Word for our day and for every day. To us it is the sole and sufficient basis for our faith and practice, and we reject all man-made doctrines that conflict with the teaching of the Word of God. In Russia, wherever I preached I presented the pastor of the church a Russian Bible. I pointed out that I could not read his and he could not read mine, but that we loved the same book and cherished the same faith. The Bible itself is a symbol of our fellowship in Christ.

We share convictions about "believers' baptism" by immersion. It was my privilege to witness a beautiful outdoor baptismal service in Limbé, Haiti, as a group of believers were buried with Christ in baptism and raised to walk with him in newness of life. This precious symbol and its deeper meaning unite Baptists around the world.

We believe in the priesthood of all believers and in salvation by grace through faith. Because of our concern for those who are lost without this faith, we believe in evangelism and missions. As John Soren well says, "The same Christ who took from our hearts the burden of sin laid on our hearts the concern to share with others the gospel that sets us free from the bondage of sin and death."

Baptists through the years have emphasized social justice and righteousness. We have emphasized brotherhood, under God, in our fellowship of believers in Christ. In Jamaica, for example, Baptists took the lead in trying to bring an end to human slavery. When the shackles were finally broken from the legs of the slaves and they were set free, many formed a procession and buried their chains in the churchyard of the Brownstown Baptist Church. They had been released from both physical and spiritual bondage through the faith the church proclaimed, and they never forgot it.

Also, Baptists have taken the lead in claiming and proclaiming full religious liberty. We believe in freedom of conscience— freedom to believe or not to believe, freedom to teach and preach the gospel we profess, freedom to own property and to publish and proclaim our faith—and with all this the right to change one's faith. Felix Manz was drowned in Zurich because of his devotion to religious liberty and believers' baptism and because he claimed freedom of conscience.

When we see what others have suffered for our faith, at the hands of both church and state, we cannot but proclaim full religious liberty for all and the separation of church and state as ideals toward which we strive.

This is our Baptist World Fellowship, embodied in the Baptist World Alliance and expressed in varied ways around the world. It is, of course, part of a far larger fellowship of all believers in Christ as Lord, but within that larger fellowship our own Baptist ties around the world grow stronger with the years.

> Blest be the tie that binds
> Our hearts in Christian love.